This item has to

Guid ——— Dyspraxia
and Developmental
Coordination Disorders

Guide to Dyspraxia and Developmental Coordination Disorders

Amanda Kirby
& Sharon Drew

 David Fulton Publishers

David Fulton Publishers
2 Park Square, Milton Park, Abingdon, Oxon OX14 4RN

270 Madison Avenue, New York, NY 10016

Transferred to digital printing

David Fulton Publishers is an imprint of the Taylor & Francis Group, an informa business

British Library Cataloguing in Publication Data
A catalogue record for this book is available from the British Library.

ISBN 1–85346–913–0

Typeset by Mark Heslington, Scarborough, North Yorkshire

Contents

Acknowledgements

This book has been written by clinicians with firsthand experience, for teachers and health professionals striving to understand more about Developmental Coordination Disorder.

The authors have been privileged to have had extensive experience of working with children and adults with DCD. They have also provided training to over 15,000 professionals in the past few years. This has allowed them to hear the views and opinions of both the 'users' and the 'providers'. It is hoped that the book will lead the reader to question and seek out answers to some of the puzzles of DCD, and offer some solutions.

Thanks must go to all the team at the Dyscovery Centre. Without their help and assistance the book could not have been written and would never have been finished. In addition, we must thank our partners who have been there to support us late at night with cups of tea when emails were flying back and forth. Also, our thanks must go to Nichola Jones and her team at Bridgend Education Authority who have worked with us extensively and have helped us to develop and practice our models of care and support.

CHAPTER 1

Introduction

This book considers Development Coordination Disorders (DCD) in the context of other specific learning difficulties. It also considers how the child or adult is recognised and managed in school or in the workplace, and the implications of the diagnosis or 'the label' being given.

It does not give all of the answers to the problems but rather allows the reader to consider the underlying difficulties, understand the deficits, critically analyse current research and practice and then consider the solutions. It is intended to invite thought and promote discussion rather than being an easy 'reach for the shelf for the answers' book.

Why diagnose/why label in the first place?

This is really dependent upon who gives the label and who wants to have a label.

A label can mean:
- Acknowledgement for the parent of worries and concerns, and confirmation of the condition: allows others to see the parent as not just 'another over-anxious parent'.
- The provision of funds or services for the child.
- The provision of a cohort of individuals with signs and symptoms that may be useful for research.
- Allowing individuals working with the child to read up around the condition and consider what type of support is required.
- It may be used in legal cases as a reference point to consider one child's support compared to others.
- It may be used to plan service delivery or for baseline assessment and in-school remediation programmes.
- It may suggest negative connotations and may mean that individuals who come into contact with the child have preconceived ideas about the strengths and difficulties based on their experience of others with the same label they have come into contact with, who could even have been atypical.

- Placing children in very small boxes and not seeing them from all perspectives – this may lead to missing a diagnosis.
- The child perhaps ends up with many labels but not the right type of help.
- The child then being 'tattooed' for life with what they *can't* do rather than what they *can* do.
- One label does not carry as much weight as another; for instance, medical labels may seem more important than educational ones (e.g. epilepsy versus dyslexia).

Should we give diagnostic or functional labels?

So should we be giving diagnostic or functional labels to help individuals with DCD and other specific learning difficulties? Figure 1.1 contrasts diagnostic and functional labels.

Diagnostic	Functional (potential alternative descriptor)
DCD	Difficulties with ball skills, poor handwriting at speed, difficulty with dressing
Dyslexia	Spelling, reading difficulties
ADHD	Difficulty concentrating when noisy, easily distracted, impulsive
Asperger's Syndrome	Difficulty making friends, sees things literally

Figure 1.1   Diagnostic and functional labels

What conditions fall under the label of specific learning difficulties?

Specific learning difficulties include conditions such as:

- Dyslexia
- Asperger's Syndrome
- DCD (Developmental Coordination Disorder)
- ADHD (Attention Deficit Hyperactivity Disorder)
- DAMP (Deficit of Attention and Motor Perception)
- Dysgraphia
- Dyscalculia

Co-morbidity

Thought needs to be given to the extent to which there is co-morbidity or whether the above conditions overlap (see Figure 1.2).

'Co-morbidity is the rule rather than the exception' (Kaplan *et al.* 1998) – specific learning difficulties do commonly overlap with one another. Are all conditions coming from some similar root causes, all having atypical brain functioning? It is where and how in the brain the pattern of difficulties arises that leads the individual to have a range of problems which we then label accordingly.

Co-morbidity is described as a situation where two or more conditions that are diagnostically distinguishable from one another tend to occur together. The exact nature of the relationship between co-morbid conditions is a matter of some debate in the research literature (Martini *et al.* 1999). Henderson and Barnett (1998) also reviewed the labels issue and discussed the issues of classification. Gillberg in 1998 (in Landgren *et al.* 1998) looked at the overlapping nature of DCD and ADHD and the prevalence of the coexisting conditions in a population study in Sweden. In the study of all 6–7-year-old children in a Swedish community (approximately 25,000 inhabitants), 589 6–7-year-old children from the town of Mariestad were identified. Of these children, 10.7 per cent were noted to have some kind of neurodevelopmental disorder. This was broken down into the following groups: DAMP 5.3 per cent, ADHD 2.4 per cent, DCD 1.7 per cent and mental retardation (IQ less than 70) 2.5 per cent. The estimated rates were: DAMP 6.9 per cent, DCD 6.4 per cent and ADHD 4.0 per cent. All children with

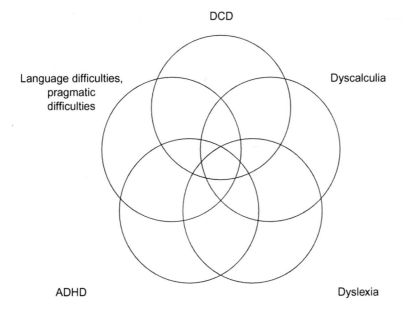

Figure 1.2 Co-morbidity/overlap

DAMP had DCD and attention deficits, and about half of them fulfilled the criteria for ADHD.

Another population study (Kaplan *et al.* 1998) also found overlap with children who had DCD, ADHD and dyslexia. Of this diagnosed group, 23 per cent were found with ADHD, DCD and dyslexia. Only 10 per cent had ADHD and DCD, and 22 per cent had dyslexia and DCD only.

It is particularly difficult to determine whether one condition is in fact a symptom of the other – causality versus correlation. These important debates aside, research provides support for a number of conditions co-occurring with learning disabilities more often than expected 'just by chance'.

The largest body of studies supports a co-morbid relationship between learning difficulties (usually termed learning disabilities in the US) and attention deficit disorder (with or without hyperactivity). This extensive research, featuring co-morbidity estimates as high as 70 per cent, was summarised recently by Riccio *et al.* (1994).

A large percentage of those who have ADHD also have accompanying learning difficulties, while approximately 30 per cent of those who have learning difficulties also have ADHD.

A group of disorders also found frequently to be co-morbid with learning difficulties is that involving social, emotional, and/or behavioural difficulties. Studies suggest that anywhere from 24 to 52 per cent of students with learning difficulties have some form of such a disorder (Rock *et al.* 1997). This group encompasses diagnoses such as conduct disorder and oppositional/defiant disorder (Shaywitz and Shaywitz 1991). Research also suggests that depressive or dysthymic disorders co-occur with learning difficulties (San Miguel *et al.* 1996) although the nature of the relationship continues to be controversial and requires further research. This is discussed more fully later in the book.

A recent report in the *British Medical Journal* (June 2002) showed that in the US 7 per cent of the childhood population has ADHD, with half supposed to have an associated 'other learning disability'. There is difficulty comparing figures because different terminology is used in different countries and so there is a lack of consistency in what specialists are measuring.

Research provides significant evidence supporting the co-morbidity of ADHD with the following disorders: Tourette's Syndrome, schizophrenia, epilepsy, language/communication disorders (Riccio *et al.* 1994) and Developmental Co-ordination Disorder (Martini *et al.* 1999, Missiuna and Polatajko 1995).

What is the evidence for co-morbidity in DCD?

The difficulty of counting 'clean' populations that do not have a mixed profile has been discussed time and again by researchers. Other research work completed by

Martini *et al.* (1999), Henderson and Barnett (1998), and Clarkin and Kendall (1992), has discussed how difficult it is to determine whether one condition is in fact a symptom of another.

The same quandary is seen if you look at material written by the specific learning disability charities such as the BDA, I-CAN, the Dyslexia Institute, and AFASIC, to name a few. You may be confused to see similar symptoms and signs for differing conditions such as ADHD, dyslexia, DCD and Asperger's Syndrome. It seems that one disorder 'pinches' symptoms and signs from another. Is the reason for this that we tend to assess only bits of the child in isolation, and tend not to look at the 'whole' child? The label is sometimes determined by which service the child and family access.

It is important to diagnose these underlying difficulties accurately in order to decide how to help remediate and support the child. This then enables and informs the education system how to create and develop an appropriate Individual Education Plan (IEP) for the child. Accurate diagnosis leads to accurate intervention plans tailored to the specific needs of the child and not packaged neatly to fit the label.

How do we define DCD?

DSM-IV Sourcebook American Psychiatric Association Diagnostic and Statistical Manual (DSM-IV)

Diagnostic features
The essential features of Developmental Coordination Disorder are:

(Criterion A) A marked impairment in the development of motor coordination.

(Criterion B) The diagnosis is made only if this impairment significantly interferes with academic achievement or activities of daily living.

(Criterion C) The diagnosis is made if the coordination difficulties are not due to a general medical condition (e.g. cerebral palsy, hemiplegia, or muscular dystrophy) and the criteria are not met for Pervasive Developmental Disorder.

(Criterion D) If mental retardation is present, the motor difficulties are in excess of those usually associated with it.

The manifestations of this disorder vary with age and development. For example, younger children may display clumsiness and delays in achieving development motor milestones (e.g. walking, crawling, sitting, tying shoelaces, buttoning shirts, zipping pants). Older children may display difficulties with the motor aspects of assembling puzzles, building models, playing ball, and printing or writing. The adult may have fewer of the fine motor difficulties but be left with handwriting and organisational problems.

Associated features and disorders

- Problems commonly associated with Developmental Coordination Disorder include delays in other non-motor milestones. (This is discussed in greater detail in later chapters.)
- Developmental Coordination Disorder must be distinguished from motor impairments that are due to a general medical condition.
- Problems in coordination may also be associated with specific neurological disorders (e.g. cerebral palsy, progressive lesions of the cerebellum, lesions in the brain such as tumour, muscular dystrophy), but in these cases there is definite neural damage and abnormal findings on neurological examination.
- If moderate to severe learning disability is present, Developmental Coordination Disorder can be diagnosed *only* if the motor difficulties are in excess of those usually associated with the level of learning disability.
- A diagnosis of Developmental Coordination Disorder is not given if the criteria are met for a Pervasive Developmental Disorder.

What is the incidence of DCD?

This has been estimated to be as high as 6 per cent for children in the age range of 5–11 years.

Kadesjo and Gillberg (1998) examined all seven-year-old children in one city and found that 7.3 per cent had moderate to severe DCD, with a boy:girl ratio of 5.3:1. The percentage has varied in different studies but is usually around 6 per cent, depending on what cut-offs are being used.

Is there a difference between Dyspraxia and DCD?

DCD has been defined as in the DSM1V criteria. Jean Ayres (1965) defined Developmental Dyspraxia as a disorder of sensory integration interfering with the ability to plan and execute skilled non-habitual tasks. Gubbay (1985) talked about the child as a clumsy child whose ability to perform skilled movement is impaired despite normal intelligence and normal findings on neurological examination. Cermak (Cermak *et al.* 2002) defined dyspraxia as a difficulty in planning and carrying out motor acts in a correct sequence. Neuropsychiatric definitions consider dyspraxia to be a problem with conceptualisation and planning of gestures and sequences.

The child with dyspraxia has a praxis/planning problem and does not know what to do and how to move, whereas the child with DCD has difficulties with coordination and execution. The latter child knows what to do but does not do it very well (Burton and Miller 1998). Is this true and does it make a difference in the way you approach treatment and support the child? There is ongoing debate whether clinicians can really tell the difference between the two labels. At the DCD V international conference in Banff in 2002, there was consensus over using the term DCD and dropping the term dyspraxia altogether.

There is some difficulty with this in the UK where there is additional confusion, as the term dyspraxia is now often used in the media, by teachers and by many health professionals to mean all children with coordination difficulties, regardless of whether any diagnostic criteria have been applied (Henderson and Barnett 1998). We have to accept to some degree that this will continue, as dyspraxia has now become another 'Dys......'. If we are to be purists and consider which terms to use, we do need to make sure we are all considering the same children. If we consider a therapeutic approach, then this should be determined by the underlying difficulty, and evidence-based principles in terms of what has been shown to work and what has not; this includes both psychological and pharmacological therapies.

If we have a functional approach then this is less of an issue as we are being child-led and addressing the functional difficulties wherever they occur. However, we need to review whether intervention is working, and modify it accordingly to gain the best response for the child.

Implications for assessment/diagnosis

A proper and detailed assessment of a child's profile of neurodevelopmental strengths and difficulties is a critical step in devising an effective plan for his or her management at home and in school. The following general principles can guide the assessment process:

- Health professionals and educationalists need to understand the key specific learning difficulties, what the signs and symptoms are, and have some under-standing of the underlying mechanisms for functioning.
- The assessment process should stress the search for strengths as well as outline the difficulties in such a way that this can be translated into giving practical help or remediation or appropriate therapy, i.e. strong intellectual orientation toward certain subject matter.
- Information should be gathered through a process of formal testing and clin-ical observations and gathered from a number of viewpoints (e.g. from home, school, from the children's centre) to ensure a balanced and objective diag-nosis is made.
- Depending on the complexity of the child, the assessment should be made by a multidisciplinary team if possible. This should be in several stages:
  ○ Observation from parents and teachers – with some guidance in the areas of information required

- ○ Evaluation by a health professional to consider any other underlying neurological causes for dysfunction
  - ○ Evaluation by the multidisciplinary team
  - ○ Evaluation at school/community setting to gain further information or confirm diagnosis.
- It is important to seek patterns that are evident in the observations and/or tests of more than one individual and across time. This increases the likelihood of a correct diagnosis, e.g. certain behaviour may be seen as a consequence of asking a child to write in different classes, but is different when he or she is asked to write on a computer at home.
- The reports should contain information on potential diagnosis if this is appropriate, as well as implications for home and for school, and guidance about therapeutic intervention or practical advice to ameliorate the difficulties.

Implications for management

The successful management of a child with specific learning difficulties requires a multifaceted, coordinated approach. The parents, teachers, and any involved professionals need to seek common goals for the child and must communicate these between them. This is one of the most difficult aspects of management as assessments may be completed at different times and places and make good communication hard to achieve. There is also at present differing levels of understanding and expectations regarding what health professionals can give in terms of therapeutic intervention, and what the education system is able to give in terms of manpower and resources.

A child, although having common labels, will have differing needs and a tailored programme of support has to be the gold standard.

The information/report from the assessment should:

- Lack jargon – this is difficult when the report may be written for differing audiences, but must be achieved to demystify what is wrong and what needs to be done, without oversimplifying and over-diluting the information.
- Highlight where a strategy or aid needs to be put in place to bypass the difficulty rather than trying to overcome it, e.g. use of laptop.
- Show how improvement should be measured and show the steps required to seek improvement.
- Give an indication where there may be difficulties in the future and when review may be required.
- Indicate if further assessment by other agencies is required.

- Associated problems such as peer relationships, low self-esteem, family dysfunction and co-morbid conditions should be specifically addressed in the individualised management plan.
- Treatment should be multi-modal and involve consideration of simultaneous medication use, behaviour management, family counselling and support, educational management, and specific developmental issues.

This book takes the reader through the underlying difficulties of DCD, assessment tools, identification of the individual at different stages of his or her life and considers management of the difficulties in the context of home and the working environment, whether at school or for the adult in the workplace.

References

Ayres, A.J. (1965) 'Patterns of perceptual-motor dysfunction in children: a factor analytic study', *Perceptual and Motor Skills*, **20**, 335–68.

Burton, A. and Miller, D. (1998) *Movement Skill Assessment*, Chap. 3). Champaign, IL: Human Kinetics.

Cermak, S.A., Gubbay, S.S. and Larkin, D. (2002) 'What is Developmental Coordination Disorder?' in S.A. Cermak and D. Larkin (eds), *Developmental Coordination Disorder*, pp. 2–22. Albany, NY: Delmar.

Clarkin, J.F. and Kendall, P.C. (1992) 'Comorbidity and treatment planning: summary and future directions', *Journal of Consulting and Clinical Psychology*, **60**, 904–8.

Decker, S.L., McIntosh, D.E., Kelly, A.M., Nicholls, S.K. and Dean, R.S. (2001) 'Comorbidity among individuals classified with attention disorders', *International Journal of Neuroscience*, **110** (1–2), 43–54.

Gillberg, C. (1998) 'Hyperactivity, inattention and motor control problems: prevalence, co-morbidity and background factors', *Folia Phoniatrica et Logopaedica*, **50**, 107–17.

Gubbay, S.S. (1985) 'Clumsiness', in P.J. Vinken, G.W. Bruyn and H.L. Klawans (eds), *Handbook of Clinical Neurology*, pp. 159–67. New York: Elsevier.

Gubbay, S.S. (1978) 'The management of developmental apraxia', *Developmental Medicine and Child Neurology*, **20**, 643–6.

Henderson, S.E. and Barnett, A.L. (1998) 'The classification of specific motor coordination disorders in children: some problems to be solved', *Human Movement Science*, **17**, 449–69.

Kadesjö, B. and Gillberg, C. (1998) 'Attention deficits and clumsiness in Swedish seven-year-old children', *Developmental Medicine and Child Neurology*, **40**, 796–804.

Kaplan, B.J., Wilson, B.N., Dewey, D. and Crawford, S.G. (1998) 'DCD may not be a discrete disorder', *Journal of Human Movement Science*, 17, 471–90.

Landgren, M., Kjellman, B. and Gillberg, C. (1998) 'Attention deficit disorder with developmental coordination disorders', *Archives of Disease in Childhood*, 79 (3), 207–12.

Martini, R., Heath, N. and Missiuna, C. (1999) 'A North American analysis of the relationship between learning disabilities and developmental coordination disorder', *International Journal of Learning Disabilities*, 14, 46–58.

Missiuna, C. and Polatajko, H. (1995) 'Developmental dyspraxia by any other name: are they all just clumsy children?', *American Journal of Occupational Therapy*, 49 (7), 619–27.

Riccio, C.A., Hynd, G.W., Cohen, M.J., Hall, J. and Molt, L.F. (1994) 'Comorbidity of central auditory processing disorder and attention deficit hyperactivity disorder', *Journal of the American Academy of Child and Adolescent Psychiatry*, 33 (6), 849–57.

Rock, E.E., Fessler, M.A. and Church, R.P. (1997) 'The concomitance of learning disabilities and emotional/behavioral disorders: a conceptual model', *Journal of Learning Disabilities*, 30 (3), 245–63.

San Miguel, S.K., Forness, S.R. and Kavale, K.A. 'Social skills deficits in learning disabilities – the psychiatric comorbidity hypothesis', *Learning Disability Quarterly*, 19, Fall, 1996.

Shaywitz, B.A. and Shaywitz, S.E. (1991) 'Comorbidity: a critical issue in attention deficit disorder', *Journal of Child Neurology*, 6, Supplement, S13–22.

CHAPTER 2

Developmental Coordination Disorder – nature or nurture?

Learning objectives
- To understand the key elements of the neurology of the brain and how these relate to DCD.
- To consider the underlying causes of DCD.
- To critically evaluate current knowledge, comparing and contrasting the different effects that environment and genetics may have on each other.
- To analyse current research and consider how this may impact on the child in school and at home.

Learning outcomes
To be able to consider the current thinking and theories, and the impact these have on practice across all disciplines, and how this may affect your working practices with parents.

Introduction

This chapter aims to cover the basic neurology as well as consider the diagnostic difficulties in using the term DCD.

To understand what difficulties children have with DCD we also need to consider what may have caused them at brain level and even at the level of the cells and hormones in the body. It is therefore necessary to have a basic understanding of the normal development of the brain and the central nervous system, and its anatomy and function. Some of these mechanisms are understood and some of them are mere postulations at this stage, as further research is required to understand at a gross anatomical, cellular and biochemical level the processes that may be occurring.

It is up to each reader to consider the theories proposed and decide whether the model stands up to scrutiny, and, even more importantly, will stand the test of time.

What is DCD?

- DCD is not a disease; we cannot catch it.
- There are no blood tests like those for diabetes.
- It is a symptom collection, i.e. you look at what the child can and cannot do compared with the normal population and see if they are at one end of the spectrum.
- There are no clear cut-offs, i.e. standard criteria that are used across the UK, so that in different areas professionals are using different tools to measure and assess the child and diagnose.
- There is no single cause for DCD.
- There will be a number of factors influencing a child's outcome: as with all children there is the effect of both nature and nurture.
- There will be no single cure!

This chapter tries to unravel some of these influences and how they may interrelate.

It would be simplistic to think that there is one area of the brain that is 'the problem' in DCD and if we knew where that was we would have the answer. The interaction between different areas of the brain at both the tissue and cell level makes understanding complex and research difficult. However, this chapter considers current thinking on the areas that may be affected in DCD.

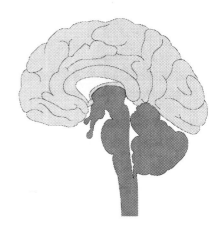

Which areas do we need to consider?

The brain develops as an integrated whole: anatomy, physiology, biochemistry all develop together. Unfortunately, the ways of studying brain development have to make artificial divisions into methods of studying *structural* development, and methods of studying *functional* development. Quite often there seems to be little clear relationship between the two. As new techniques are opening up a whole new and exciting world of functional neuro-imaging, where pictures of the inside of the brain are at photo-quality, e.g. with magnetic resonance imaging (MRI) and

Positron Emission Technology (PET), the relationship of function to structure can start to be seen in the live adult or child.

Is DCD a congenital or acquired disorder?

How do we unravel what causes DCD? As we have said that DCD is not a disease but a symptom complex, it must ultimately have causes, whether congenital or acquired or a combination of the two. It has been well accepted that the brain is the 'heart' of learning. Difficulties in coordination are going to have a neurological basis, a genetic influence and an environmental influence.

Do individuals with DCD have specific genes that confer increased likelihood?

We know from some research completed in the area of dyslexia that about 50 per cent of the individuals concerned have some genetic basis for the condition and certainly there has been some research to isolate genes that predispose to dyslexia (Fisher *et al.* 2002, Grigorenko 2001).

Is DCD a hormonal condition?

We know that specific hormones control motor movements. In Parkinson's disease, Dopamine is decreased and this produces cogwheel rigidity and difficulties with initiating and carrying out smooth movements.

What chemicals circulate in the brain and could some of these be deficient in DCD, or could the receptors be less responsive?

Dopamine – Dopamine is the principal neurotransmitter that mediates a wide range of brain functions, including locomotion, emotion, learning, and neuroendocrine modulation. It controls arousal levels and is important for physical motivation. In Parkinson's disease, levels become depleted and sufferers find it hard to initiate movement and to carry out smooth movements. It also has an effect on mood disturbance. Under-activity can cause depression and lethargy, social withdrawal and lack of attention and concentration. (Serotonin and noradrenaline also play a part in this as well.) Has Dopamine an effect in individuals with DCD? Studies with mice provide genetic evidence that Dopamine is essential for controlling spontaneous and voluntary movement and emotional learning (Kobayashi and Sano 2000).

Serotonin – This has an important role in anxiety and mood. It also affects sleep, pain and appetite.

Acetylcholine – This controls attention, learning and memory.

Noradrenaline – This controls arousal and mood.

Glutamate – Helps link neurons and affects learning and long-term memory.

Encephalins and endorphins – These affect alterations in mood, stress and pain.

At the moment we are unsure which chemical messengers are involved but further research may specifically target these chemicals and may make it possible to have medication in the future to treat DCD.

Is DCD due to neurological delay?

Is DCD due to neurological delay, implying that it may catch up over time, or neurological deviancy, implying a lesion or disconnection in the brain? There is some evidence to show that some children may display an absolute lag and not just a reduced rate of progress, i.e. in time, the children will not just catch up with their peers (Barnett and Henderson 1992).

Is DCD seen more because of environmental changes?

We know that environmental factors can also have a major effect on our ability to learn. This can be seen at the prenatal, perinatal and postnatal stages. In addition, early years physical and emotional abuse can have a lasting effect on a child's behaviour. Certainly dietary changes over the last 30 years may also have a significant effect on the number of children having coordination and other related specific learning difficulties (Richardson and Ross 2000).

Parts of the brain and spinal cord, and their functions

Let us first consider the anatomy of the brain to try and understand further where difficulties may occur.

The brain

There are two sides to the brain, the right and left, joined by the corpus callosum (Figure 2.1).

The Structure

- Right hemisphere – controls emotion. The right brain tends to see the whole and is able to integrate sensory and emotional stimuli. It is also able to make connections, e.g. with humour, and it is more sensitive to negative emotions.

- Left hemisphere – This is the area where analytical, logical and time-sensitive information is dealt with, and tends to see the details. It is more associated with happiness.
- Corpus callosum – The cerebral hemispheres are joined by the corpus callosum. There is transfer of information back and forth across the two sides of the brain. The corpus callosum is larger in females than in males. This may be

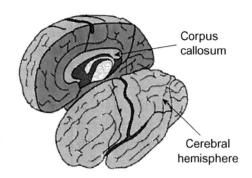

Figure 2.1   Structure of the brain

the reason why there are more boys seen with specific learning difficulties than girls, as their brains may be less easily able to compensate for a difficulty in one side of the brain. Sigmundsson (1998) has postulated there may be a problem with the corpus callosum in transferring information from one side of the brain to the other. There has been other research in dyslexia showing a difference in growth patterns in this area. Could this be happening also in DCD?

Difference between males and females	
Males	**Females**
Better at mathematical reasoning tasks	Better at language tasks
Better at figure ground activities	Faster at language development
Easier to rotate objects	Better at empathy and social interaction
Better at hitting targets	Better at matching items Better at generating ideas

It is interesting to note in individuals with DCD/Asperger's, that the left-sided type activities are preserved but the right-sided activities are often the ones that are impaired. It is also of interest that the sex ratios mean the incidence of DCD is far greater in males than females. There is some evidence to show that males produce fewer in terms of over-production of nerve cells, and do not cope as well as females if there is early brain injury in utero (Bryden *et al.* 1995, see Brain Cognition 1995 in the References). They do not seem to be able to compensate as well.

- The brain stem – This contains nuclei, and controls automatic activity; that is, without the control of the brain in the reticular formation (e.g. respiration, digestion). Someone can be 'brain dead' but still their body can breathe with control from the brain stem.
- Cerebellum – The brain stem has nuclei that control and monitor gravity and movement in the inner ear. The cerebellum is located around the brain stem and its role is organising gravity, movement, and muscle joint sensations. This enables individuals to make smooth movements. Someone with cerebellar difficulties will be seen to have a fine tremor and not be able to do a movement known as dysdiadochokinesia. This is the smooth movement of being able to turn one hand back and forth over the other one. There is some evidence that cerebellar disorders are seen in greater numbers in dyslexic individuals than in the main population.

Cerebral hemispheres

The cerebral hemispheres plan and perform an action by the body:

- The cortex – this is the outer layer – different areas – visual perception, speech, body movements.
- The corticospinal tract is known to be responsible for fine highly skilled movements.

The four lobes crudely control different aspects of bodily functions (see Figure 2.2):

- The frontal lobe controls emotion. Lack of activity is often seen in the pre-frontal cortex in depression.
- The parietal lobe controls somatic sensation from the thalamus. This is called astereognosis – and acts by integrating the senses.
- The temporal lobe controls auditory stimuli, understanding of sound, speech mechanisms.
- The occipital lobe controls recognition and integration of visual stimuli.

The limbic system controls emotional responses and has several parts to it. These are:

- The thalamus – this relays information for further processing.
- The hypothalamus – this is below the thalamus and controls the body's environment. Different parts of the hypothalamus have differing roles in control.

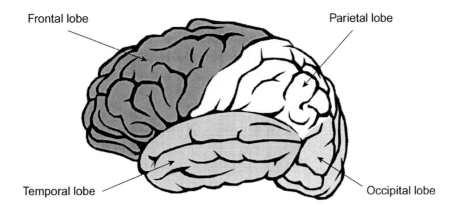

Frontal lobe

Parietal lobe

Temporal lobe

Occipital lobe

Figure 2.2 The four lobes

Individuals with anorexia may have impaired functioning. It seems likely that this is a neurotransmitter difficulty, with overactivity of serotonin, which has an effect on mood and appetite.

- The hippocampus – this is essential for laying down long-term memory.
- The amygdala – this is where fear and other emotional stimuli are registered. One part of the amygdala responds to facial expressions (right amygdala) and another to tone of voice (left amygdala). 'Fight and flight' take place in this area – quick responses occur first and the frontal cortex then modulates these. The frontal cortex checks the context and makes a decision if action needs to take place. If the decision by the cortex is to dampen things down and not to react, the brain sends signals to the hypothalamus and then to the amygdala. This is why in very young children the quick response is the usual one seen, as their frontal cortex has not been fully developed, so the response is primarily only coming from the amygdala without any control. Most children also get better at recognising facial expressions as they get older and as their frontal lobes mature. It is also known that poor frontal cortex functioning may be linked to aggression in response to stimuli where the frontal cortex fails to dampen down the reaction.
- The putamen – looks after automatic movements that have been learned by repetition and keeps them flowing. It is interesting to note that in Tourette's Syndrome, the putamen has been seen as being overactive and the caudate nucleus, which is close to the amygdala, is overactive in Obsessional Compulsive Disorder. The caudate nucleus looks after automatic thinking. These conditions have been seen to be concurrent with other conditions such as ADHD as well as DCD.

The spinal cord

The spinal cord carries messages to and from the brain and regulates functions of the internal organs. It does not have a role for sensory integration but carries signals to and from the brain.

Is DCD caused by a 'fault' in an area of the brain?

There is evidence that specific areas of the brain control motor coordination. The cerebellum is the area of the brain that controls balance and smooth movements, the pre-frontal motor cortex has a role in producing movements, and the hypothalamus controls temperature regulation as well as controlling hormones that are released by the pituitary gland.

The cerebellum is important for motor control and in perception of time, both of which are usually problematic for the individual with DCD (Nicolson *et al.* 1999, Ivry 1993).

The hypothalamus influences the autonomic control, heat control and has an effect on the hormones and other neurotransmitters in the body. Some children with DCD do seem to have a problem with thermoregulatory function, which may be due to a lack of control in the hypothalamus.

Recent research into early brain development and dyslexia, and how this may relate to DCD

Some researchers believe that too many brain cells are produced during normal development. There are various estimates that not just connections but 15–85 per cent of cells themselves die as a part of remodelling during development, although there is no very good evidence that massive neuronal 'die back' occurs under normal circumstances in man.

One theory is that early in development, certain areas of the brain may not be committed to definite functions, and damage to an area which would have performed a particular function is compensated for by that function being transferred to another area, either on the same side or on the opposite side of the brain. However, later, quite small lesions in important places can have quite devastating results.

Professor John Stein has found that in dyslexics, the development of the visual magnocellular system is impaired: development of the magnocellular layers of the dyslexic lateral geniculate nucleus (LGN) is abnormal: this then makes their motion sensitivity reduced.

Good magnocellular function is essential for high motion sensitivity and stable binocular fixation (seeing with two eyes together). The cerebellum is the head ganglion of magnocellular systems. Thus, there is

Granule Cell

---

evidence that most reading problems may have a fundamental sensorimotor cause. It is considered that the dysfunction is also similar in DCD.

There has been a clear genetic basis for impaired development of magnocells throughout the brain. The development of magnocells may be impaired by autoanti-bodies affecting the developing brain. Magnocells also need high amounts of polyun-saturated fatty acids to preserve the membrane flexibility that permits the rapid conformational changes of channel proteins which underlie their transient sensitivity, and this is where there may be a link between nutrition and brain developmental prob-lems that we see. (Stein 1991)

So where and when may problems occur that lead to the child having DCD?

1. Prenatal – is development different at this stage?
   (a) Influenced by maternal nutrition
   (b) Early movements of the baby in the womb

2. Prenatal – genetic influence

3. Prenatal or perinatal – infection occurring in the baby

4. Perinatal – ischaemia (lack of oxygen)

5. Perinatal – trauma due to delivery mechanism, e.g. forceps

6. Postnatal impact
   (a) Influence in the development of cognition and memory
   (b) Influence of nutrition on the child
   (c) Immunisation
   (d) Environmental effects

---

1. Prenatal

(a) Influenced by maternal nutrition

The correct environment for growth and development is affected by maternal nutrition as well as perinatal conditions (around the birth). The mother may have poor nutrition and a diet low in essential fatty acids, and this can have an effect on the development of the nervous system. Either a hormone deficiency or nutritional deficiency can have a direct impact on the developing foetus and can affect phys-ical and cognitive development. The stage of the insult may determine the type of impact that may occur. Folic acid deficiency can cause spina bifida. It is thought that folate is crucial to the foetus in the first 12 weeks of development. We also know that alcoholic mothers can cause a condition in the baby called foetal alcohol syndrome, which leaves the baby having cognitive deficits. Hypothyroidism (under-active thyroid) in the baby (also used to be known as cretinism) can have an effect on nerve development and causes cognitive deficits as well. We now test for this at birth to make sure we identify and treat these children so that there are no long-term negative consequences.

Because much of the brain and retina are made of long-chain fatty acids, it is vital that mothers take in adequate levels, particularly during the last few months of pregnancy when foetal brain and nervous system growth are very rapid. Of interest is the fact that breastfed babies on average have an IQ eight points higher than non-breastfed. There has also been noted a direct connection between incidences of post-partum depression (associated with fatty acid depletion) and fish consumption. Where there is more fish eaten, there is less depression (Japan at 4 per cent). Less fish, more depression (UAE 26 per cent, UK about 14 per cent).There is also a link between prematurity and lack of fish consumption in the mother (Olsen *et al.* 2002).

(b) Early movements of the baby in the womb
Experiments on aborted foetuses conducted in America during the 1930s showed that foetal movements begin from six weeks and are initially reflex responses to various stimuli. Accompanying these reflex movements, electrical activity in the brain and the release of neurotransmitters have also been found to begin very early. These experiments have more recently been confirmed by foetal ultrasound, which show movements from six weeks gestation.

Are we able to identify abnormal movements in utero in the baby with DCD? Some mothers do say that their child with DCD, compared to a previous baby, was less active in the womb. This may be merely subjective and requires further studies.

2. Prenatal – genetic influence

Different genes express themselves in different ways. There are dominant, autosomal recessive and sex-linked chromosomes. So far we have not identified a specific gene related to DCD. There are likely to be a number of genes that lead to the individual having symptoms and signs of coordination and related difficulties. Examples of these are as follows, where children show some difficulties with coordination.

Dominant – for example, Ehlers-Danlos Syndrome. Ehlers-Danlos Syndrome (EDS) is a part of a group of hereditary, connective tissue disorders characterised by defects of the major structural protein in the body, collagen. Collagen, a tough, fibrous protein, plays an essential role in 'holding together', strengthening, and providing elasticity to bodily cells and tissues. Due to defects of collagen, primary EDS symptoms and findings include abnormally flexible, loose joints (articular hypermobility) that may easily become dislocated; unusually loose, thin, 'stretchy' (elastic) skin; and excessive fragility of the skin, blood vessels, and other bodily tissues and membranes. Each subtype of EDS is a distinct hereditary disorder that may affect individuals within certain families. In other words, parents with one subtype of EDS will not have children with another EDS subtype. Depending upon the specific subtype present, Ehlers-Danlos Syndrome is usually transmitted as an autosomal dominant or autosomal recessive trait. Children with Type 3, also known as benign hypermobility syndrome, may have associated difficulties with coordination as their structural framework may be more 'wobbly' than that of their peers. Other children with conditions such as Marfans disease may also have similar difficulties.

A proportion of children with Neurofibromatosis – NF1 type also have difficulties with coordination.

From this we know that certain conditions predispose to coordination difficulties. Many children with DCD do not have an identifiable cause. There is often evidence of a strong history of specific learning difficulties within the family.

In time we may find specific genes that confer an increased likelihood of difficulties with motor coordination, and we may end up having an antenatal screen to identify these. We are still at an early stage in understanding the mechanisms behind these conditions. There will be a combination of nature plus nurture at play in DCD and it is important to unravel and consider both elements.

3. Prenatal or perinatal – infection occurring in the baby

Infection at crucial times of development can have a profound effect on the baby and may cause problems leading to abortion or other difficulties, e.g. cytomegalovirus, mumps and HIV. There is no evidence at this time that this has happened to cause DCD.

4. Perinatal – ischaemia

Ischaemia (lack of oxygen) at the time of the birth can cause the child to have cerebral palsy. Cerebral palsy affects motor movements. Sometimes individuals who are thought to have DCD, when examined thoroughly are found actually to have mild cerebral palsy. However it is not thought that ischaemia has an effect on causing DCD.

5. Perinatal – trauma due to delivery mechanism

There is no evidence to show a link between perinatal trauma and DCD at the present time.

6. Postnatal impact

(a) Influence in the development of cognition and memory

What occurs in the first few years of a baby's life in terms of nurturing and nutrition may play a crucial part later in the lives of children with DCD. We know that before three years of age we have little memory, as the hippocampus, where long-term memory is stored, is still maturing until the age of ten years.

At six months, frontal lobes have developed and the first part of cognition starts, and by one year the limbic system that controls emotion is in play, shown by the type of behaviour the child displays. Prefrontal lobes are developed at around eighteen months, and the child starts to develop self-consciousness. The reticular formation and the frontal lobes do not become fully developed until after puberty and this has an effect on emotion and impulsiveness.

(b) Influence of nutrition on the child

The breastfeeding mother will be giving the child a diet rich in essential fatty acids whereas the mother who uses bottled milk may fail to provide some essential fatty acids completely. The vegetarian also has very few external sources of highly unsaturated fatty acids.

What part do fatty acids play?

- Is there a deficiency in certain fatty acids?
- There is some evidence in those with ADD and dyslexia.
- Fatty acids play an essential part in myelination.

Arachidonic acid (AA) and dihomogamma-linolenic acid (DGLA) are a part of the structure of the brain and make up 20 per cent of the brain. Eicosapentaenoic acid (EPA) and DGLA are crucial for normal brain function.

Essential fatty acids need to come from our diet and are supplied from Omega 6 (linoleic acid) and Omega 3 (linolenic acid). Highly unsaturated fatty acids are made from these precursors. If diet is altered, as has happened today where we are eating far more highly processed foods, this can block the conversion. Deficiency in some minerals and vitamins, such as zinc, can also block this. Alcohol, coffee and smoking can also have an effect.

Most children do not consume a balanced diet and are not likely to have fatty fish in their diet at least twice a week. This deficit is also compounded by a highly processed diet as well as not having a balance of vitamins and minerals, including manganese, zinc and magnesium.

Some children with neurodevelopmental disorders may have a difficulty in converting essential fatty acids to highly unsaturated fatty acids. This may be because of a problem with absorption or may be because of an enzyme deficiency.

Some children show signs that seem linked to EFA deficiency. However it is not proven yet which children would benefit from supplementation. They may present with a range of symptoms, including dry skin, dry hair, needing to drink a lot, needing to urinate a lot, dandruff and brittle nails. These children may also have some difficulties with sleep disturbance as well as a craving for some foods such as very sweet or salty foods. They may also have difficulties with attention and concentration and visual perceptual problems (Richardson and Ross 2000, Stordy 2000).

Understanding of the link between DCD and fatty acids is still at an early stage. Further detailed research is necessary before we can say which subgroups may benefit and which will not benefit at all.

(c) Immunisation
MMR/autism – there has been much debate over the link between the MMR vaccine and autism and so far the research seems not to link the two together. More research is being undertaken in this area (Taylor et al. 2002).

(d) Environmental effects
Consider the following environmental changes and the impact these may have had on the increase in the level of specific learning difficulties that we are seeing in society today in the Western world. You can see that changes in behaviour have influenced development of the child from the very first stages into school years (Berkey 2000, Robinson et al. 1993, Dorner and Grychtolik 1978).

50 years ago	Present time	Skills lost as a consequence
Maternal play at home, more family nearby	Isolated families – no models of practice	Fewer parenting skills – little play with jigsaws, singing songs
Baby in pram, on their front	Baby in push chair – on back	Baby not put in prone position
Play on floor, in garden	Not placed on floor as often	Exploring environment – not put on the floor as seen as 'dirty'

50 years ago	Present time	Skills lost as a consequence
Few pushchairs	Pushchair – child supine	Placed only supine
Car seats not used – carrycot for travel	Car seat brought into house and child left in it	Exploring – only exploring a few inches in front of child with predetermined toys chosen by parent and not by child
Baby walker – bricks and push style	Baby walker – seated style	Low-toned child sitting to walk rather than in an extended walking position
Mealtimes on a regular daily basis	Irregular snacks	Rules and consequences not as clear for the child
Cooked meals – meat and two veg	Snack eating – highly processed foods	Nutritional value of food poor
Fish on Fridays	Little fish is eaten	Essential fatty acids not being consumed
Use knife and fork	Eat with fingers	No practice learning bi-lateral integration skills
Sit at table for meal	Watch television while eating	Fewer social interaction experiences learning about jokes and metaphor
Have a conversation as a part of the family	Eat one-by-one	No sitting at the table, concentrating, balancing
Stay at table for time	No need to stay at all	Attention skills not practised
TV in one room in the house	Computers and TV in bedrooms – child removes himself	Conversation skills avoided
Play outside in the evenings	Watch TV and go on computer	Less physical activity
Board games played	Fewer board games	Turn-taking activities less practised

Conclusions and discussion

- Brain development and the workings of the brain are complicated!
- Research is still at an early stage to understand where in the brain the difficulties may be occurring.
- In the future we may be able to target specific areas and create medication to help children with DCD.
- Nutrition has a part to play, both for the mother while the baby is in the womb and while the young child is developing. In relation to school, should we be providing breakfast clubs for all children and consider bringing back the traditional school lunch with fish on Fridays?
- How does the way we teach and the expectations we have for children at a young age affect their development? Should we be considering more play for longer, and ban the computer and television until children are at least seven years old? We can see that nurture as well as nature has an important part to play in DCD.

References

Barnett, A. and Henderson, S.E.(1992) 'Some observations on the figure drawings of clumsy children', *British Journal of Educational Psychology*, 62, 341–55.

Berkey, C.S., Rockett, H.R., Field, A.E., Gillman, M.W., Frazier, A.L., Camargo, C.A. Jr and Colditz, G.A. (2000) 'Activity, dietary intake, and weight changes in a longitudinal study of preadolescent and adolescent boys and girls', *Pediatrics*, 105, E56.

Berenbaum, S.A. and Debburg, S.D. (1995) 'Evaluating the empirical support for the role of testosterone in the Geschwind-Behan-Galaburda model of cerebral lateralization: commentary on Bryden, McManus, and Bulman-Fleming', *Brain Cognition*, 27 (1), 79–83, discussion 94–7.

Dorner, G. and Grychtolik, H. (1978) 'Long-lasting ill-effects of neonatal qualitative and/or quantitative dysnutrition in the human', *Endokrinologie*, 71 (1), 81–8.

Fisher, S.E., Francks, C., Marlow, A.J., MacPhie, I.L., Newbury, D.F., Cardon, L.R., Ishikawa-Brush, Y., Richardson, A.J., Talcott, J.B., Gayan, J., Olson, R.K., Pennington, B.F., Smith, S.D., DeFries, J.C., Stein, J.F. and Monaco, A.P.

(2002) 'Independent genome-wide scans identify a chromosome 18 quantita-tive-trait locus influencing dyslexia', *Nature and Genetics*, **30** (1), 86–91.

Grigorenko, E.L. (2001) 'Developmental dyslexia: an update on genes, brains, and environments', *Journal of Child Psychology and Psychiatry*, **42** (1), 91–125.

Ivry, R. (1993) 'Cerebellar involvement in the explicit representation of temporal information', *Annals of New York Academy of Sciences*, **682**, 214–30.

Kobayashi, K. and Sano, H. (2000) 'Dopamine deficiency in mice', *Brain Development*, **22**, Supplement 1, 554–60.

Nicolson, R.I., Fawcett, A.J., Berry, E.L. *et al.* (1999) 'Association of abnormal cerebellar activation with motor learning difficulties in dyslexic adults', *Lancet*, **353**, 1662–7.

Olsen, S. *et al.* (2002) 'Eating fish may protect against preterm delivery and low birth weight', *British Medical Journal*, **324**, 23 February, 1–5.

Richardson, A.J. and Ross, M.A. (2000) 'Fatty acid metabolism in neurodevelop-mental disorder: a new perspective on associations between attention-deficit/hyperactivity disorder, dyslexia, dyspraxia and the autistic spectrum', *Prostaglandins, Leukotrienes and Essential Fatty Acids*, **63** (1/2), 1–9.

Robinson, T.N., Hammer, L.D., Killen, J.D., Maron, D.J., Barr, Taylor, C., Maccoby, N. and Farquhar, J.W. (1993) 'Does television viewing increase obesity and reduce physical activity? Cross-sectional and longitudinal analyses among adolescent girls', *Pediatrics*, **91**, 273–80.

Sigmundsson, H. (1998) 'Inter- and intra-sensory modality matching in motor-impaired children'. PhD thesis, Norwegian University of Science and Technology.

Stein, J.F. (1991) 'Hemispheric specialisation and dyslexia', *Reading and Writing*, **3**, 435–40.

Stein, J.F. (University Laboratory of Physiology, Oxford) (1994) 'Developmental dyslexia, neural timing and hemispheric lateralisation', *International Journal of Psychophysiology*, **18** (3), 241–9.

Stein, J.F. (University Laboratory of Physiology, Oxford) (2001) 'The magnocel-lular theory of developmental dyslexia', *Dyslexia*, **7** (1), 12–36.

Stordy, B.J. (2000) 'Dark adaptation, motor skills, docosahexaenoic acid, and dyslexia', *American Journal of Clinical Nutrition*, **71**, Supplement, January, 323S–326S.

Taylor, B., Miller, E. *et al.* (2002) 'Measles, mumps, and rubella vaccination and bowel problems or developmental regression in children with autism: popula-tion study', *British Medical Journal*, **324**, 393–6.

CHAPTER 3

Development of the child

Learning objectives
- To understand the developmental processes necessary for learning and behaviour.
- To consider the impact of social and cultural changes on the developing child.
- To consider the importance of play in the developing child.

Learning outcomes
- To be able to reflect upon the differences and similarities of a child with DCD against the 'normal' population and how these may affect the child in preschool and in the first few years of education.
- To be able to set appropriate targets and goals for children with DCD in accordance with their developmental abilities.
- To reflect upon the underpinning components for learning and differentiating tasks and activities accordingly.

Introduction

To understand why an individual has difficulties in Developmental Coordination Disorder it is essential to understand the basic building blocks of development. It is these milestones that will allow the teacher in the classroom to target help and support at the appropriate level.

Human development is a continuous change in behaviour throughout the life cycle, brought about by interaction between the requirements of the task, the biology of the individual and the conditions of the environment.

Human development is often studied from a compartmentalised standpoint. It is frequently studied in terms of separate areas such as language and motor development, as if development takes place in isolation. However, children develop in an integral manner and one area of development has an influence on other areas (see Figure 3.1).

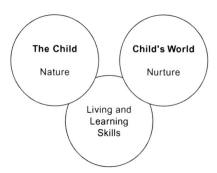

Figure 3.1   Overlap of factors which influence learning in the child

Development

Development is age-related but not age-specific. There are differences in the rate of development from one individual to another within normal limits.

The terms 'growth' and 'development' are used interchangeably, but each implies a difference in emphasis:

- growth refers to an increase in the size of an individual's body or parts during maturation;
- development refers to changes in an individual's level of functioning over a period of time.

Keogh and Sugden (1985) defined development as 'adaptive change towards competence'. Such a definition implies that throughout the life span one is required to adjust, compensate, or change in order to gain or maintain competence.

Development is therefore a continuous process encompassing all the interrelated dimensions of human existence, and care must be taken not to consider these dimensions as autonomous or limited to the growing years of childhood. Adults are every bit as involved in the developmental process as young children.

Developmental milestones play a role in our understanding of the developmental perspective on human development. These milestones represent major indexes of developmental accomplishments and are based on the average age at which children acquire certain skills or pass though certain stages (Wilson 1998).

Children with atypical developmental patterns are sometimes grouped into three general categories: delays, disorders and giftedness. Individual children may experience just one or a combination of these conditions.

- Delays – This refers to those children who experience delayed or slow progress in reaching developmental milestones in one or more areas of development such as communication, cognition, adaptive behaviour (feeding, dressing), physical and social/emotional development. The extent of the delay is determined by comparing the child's actual performance level with his or her chronological age.

- Disorders – This refers to a condition which disrupts or changes the order of a child's developmental progress. A disorder differs from a delay in that a child with a developmental delay falls significantly behind developmental norms but still proceeds through a normal sequence of development. A child with a disorder will not experience the same order of development in one or more of the developmental domains.
- Giftedness – This refers to those children who perform significantly above the norm or have the potential for such performance. Early recognition is as important for these children as it is for those with a delay or disorder as these children are at risk of poor self-concept, development of behavioural problems and underachievement.

Child development follows a natural sequence. Some children develop faster and some more slowly, but all travel pretty much the same path. In the sequence of development, the child builds on each new skill learned to develop the next more complex skill. The child practises each activity over and over again in order to master each motor and sensory element. Skills learnt are all closely interrelated.

At birth a baby is floppy with no voluntary control over its movements. This is known as the reflexive stage, where basically the lower centres of the brain are more highly developed than the motor cortex. These brain centres are capable of causing involuntary reactions to a variety of stimuli of varying intensity and duration. These reflexes serve as the primary means by which the infant is able to gather information, seek nourishment and find protection through movement.

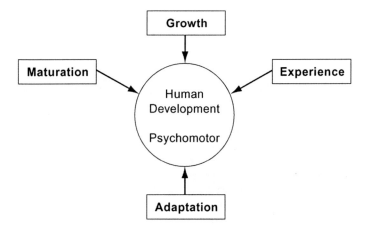

Figure 3.2   Components of human development

As the infant grows and matures during the first six months of life the central nervous system also matures and more sophisticated regions of the brain supersede these 'primitive reflexes'. Examples of reflexes are the sucking reflex and grasp reflex. These reflexes are all very important for survival in the first months of birth. Some of the reflexes we are born with disappear quickly as they are no longer required. Some emerge later after the baby is born and are necessary building blocks for movement skills, for example:

- Symmetrical Tonic Neck Reflex (STNR) – This reflex essentially emerges around 9–11 months after birth and is suppressed at about one year. It has a very short but significant life because if it remains, the infant is unable to master crawling on hands and knees.
- Asymmetrical Tonic Neck Reflex (ATNR) – This reflex emerges at around 18 weeks in the womb and is suppressed between 6–8 months after birth. This reflex fulfils many purposes:
  ○ First, training ground for eye-hand coordination. When a baby is born it can only focus its eyes at about eight inches. Outside of that the baby can see movement and shadow, but it cannot focus.
  ○ The baby slowly extends the vision from near point fixation to distance.
  ○ It enables rolling.

Summary of development				
	Prone (on tummy)	**Supine** (on back)	**Sitting**	**Standing**
0–6 weeks	• Head turns to clear airway • Buttocks high with hips and knees flexed under body, arms close to the body, elbows flexed and hands fisted	• Reflex turning head to one side with the limbs on the face side extending and the opposite limbs flexing	Pulled to sit: • Marked head lag present • Spine curved forwards in one curve	
6 weeks–3 months	• Lies on tummy • Lifts head off floor with increasing strength	• Holds head more in the midline • Limbs move symmetrically • Hands open, brought together in finger play		• Held standing • Sags at the knees

3–6 months	• Lifts head and chest higher as the stability improves around the shoulder girdle • Supports weight on flat hands and extended arms	• Lifts head from pillow 4.5 months and moves limbs vigorously • Reaches for toys • Lifts legs upright • Grips feet, approximately 6 months • Stretches arms to be lifted	Pulled to sit: • Braces shoulders and assists • Head is well controlled • The spine is straight; sits with support (5.5 months)	Held in standing: • Takes weight on extended legs • Bounces vigorously • Downward parachute obtainable
6–9 months	• Attempts to crawl (7–8 months) • Rolls over front to back (6 months) and back to front (6.5 months)	• Dislikes position unless sleepy or actively playing with toys/using hands	• Pulls self to sit; sits on floor supporting weight on arms without support • Reaches for toys in front, upward and to the side without falling over (9 months)	Pulls to stand: • Using the furniture but cannot let self down so falls down with a bump • Attempts to crawl (8 months onwards) • Forward parachute obtainable (7 months)
9–12 months			• Sits on floor for long periods of time, reaches for toys in front, to the side, upwards and can pivot to reach toy behind • Can sit from lying on back (12 months) • Crawls rapidly (12 months) and may crawl upstairs	• Pulls to stand and cruises around furniture; can lower down to floor safely while holding on • Walks with hand(s) held (11–12 months)
12–15 months				• Can walk alone but has a wide-based, uneven gait; arms are held upwards as a counter-balance; tumbles frequently; rapidly gains skill with practice • Kneels on floor alone or with slight support • Crawls upstairs but not downstairs

	Prone (on tummy)	**Supine** (on back)	**Sitting**	**Standing**
15–18 months				• Walks well and often runs; can stop and start safely • Pulls and pushes large wheeled toys • Can now crawl downstairs and backwards • Walks upstairs with hands held • Can stop to pick up toys and stand back up again • Backs or slides sideways into a small chair to sit down but climbs forward into an adult chair and turns around
2 years				• Runs at will, stopping and starting safely • Walks up and down stairs safely with hand on wall and two feet to a step • Usually crawls downstairs until 3–4 months later • Squats to play • Climbs on to furniture
2.5 years				• Climbs easy nursery apparatus • Sits on pedal cycle and steers but uses feet on floor to scoot along
3 years				• Walks upstairs with alternating feet, downstairs two feet to one step • Can walk on tiptoe • Climbs nursery apparatus easily and can peddle tricycle to turn wide corners

4 years				• Walks up and down stairs one foot to each step • Runs on tiptoe • Climbs ladders, trees and playground equipment
5 years				• Can walk along a chalk line • Runs up and down stairs • Climbs trees, etc. • Performs 'stunts' • Stands on one foot for 8–10 seconds (with arms folded 3–4 seconds) • Hops and skips on one foot

Understanding the sequence of development and the significance of sensory and motor components, it becomes easier to recognise factors that may promote success or failure in skill acquisition.

Sensory and motor components

The basic sensory and motor components that influence learning and behaviour are:

1. Body awareness
2. Coordinating body sides
3. Motor planning
4. Perception of movement
5. Fine motor control
6. Touch
7. Visual skills
8. Language processing

1. Body awareness

Receptors located in the muscles and joints tell the brain when and how the muscles are contracting or stretching, and when and how the joints are moving. This information enables the brain to know where each part of the body is and how it is travelling through space, without the need to look. The muscles, joints and brain provide each other with vital sensory information that makes postural and spatial adjustments in movement possible. This enables the execution of gross and fine motor activities, requiring subtle variations in posture, strength and dexterity.

The ability to discriminate left and right is considered to be an internal sub-component of body awareness. It is related to the spatial dimension of the body and consists of:

- Laterality – This is the awareness that the body has two distinct sides, but not the ability to label. That is a later skill. A child is increasingly aware of left and right between four and five years of age.
- Right/left discrimination – This can be defined as the ability to spontaneously label or identify the left from the right dimensions. It is not associated with handedness.
- Crossing the body midline – This reflects the degree of bilateral integration, i.e. the ability to use the two sides of the body together.
- Other spatial dimensions – Awareness of up/down, front, side, back. Concepts of front and back develop right and left.

A child with poor awareness of body parts will tend to rely more heavily on visual information in order to carry out functional tasks or move and navigate space within the environment. This is especially so if the child cannot clearly see where their arms and legs are. The child may have a vague awareness of his or her position in space, but without constantly checking visually, the child may, for example, frequently fall off their chair or have difficulty dressing. Furthermore, the

child may experience difficulty with fine motor control as they do not have adequate sensation which tells them how or where their arms/hands/fingers are moving. This then will affect the child's ability to use tools such as pencils and scissors in their hands. To the observer the child may therefore appear sloppy, clumsy or disorganised.

Information regarding body awareness is provided, when muscles and joints are working against gravity or resistance, e.g. crawling, climbing, pushing and pulling.

DEVELOPMENT OF BODY PERCEPTION IN CHILDREN	
	Perceptions
0–2 years	Can often identify gross body parts verbally Can touch 'tummy', back, arm, or leg when asked Seems aware of toes before legs
2–3 years	Becomes aware of front, back, side, head, feet Can locate objects relative to these body references Gains awareness of other body parts – thumb, hand, feet
4 years	Becomes aware that there are two sides of the body; knows their names but not the location More detailed awareness of body parts – can name little finger and first finger
5 years	Knows there is a left and right side of the body – but confused with location Can locate self to relative objects and objects to self Trunk appears in drawings
6 years	Begins to distinguish left and right body parts Becomes aware of little finger and ring finger and can name them
7–8 years	Concepts of laterality well established Begins to distinguish the left and right of others and can correctly name their left and right movements Facial expressions appear in drawings Limbs are filled in drawings and details appear in figure drawings
9–10 years	Adopts other individual's perspective with ease Can describe the arrangements of objects from another's viewpoint
Source: Cratty 1970	

2. Coordinating body sides

The ability to coordinate the right and left sides of the body and to cross the mid-line of the body is an indication that both sides of the brain are working well together and sharing information efficiently and effectively. Coordination of the two body sides is an important foundation for the development of gross and fine motor skills, enabling cerebral specialisation for skilled use of a dominant hand. It is an important foundation, for example in skills such as writing and cutting with scissors. Difficulties may present with:

- Poor coordination of the two body sides. A child may be seen to move their body to avoid crossing the mid-line, e.g. using his or her right hand to reach across and pick up something placed to the left. They may not be able to coordinate one hand moving while the other hand is stabilising during an activity, e.g. cutting with scissors. They may swap hands during a fine motor task because they are frustrated at their inability to use their hands together in a skilled way.
- Poor manipulation of toys such as beads and construction sets, and through skipping, rhythm games and riding bikes.

3. Motor planning

Motor planning is the ability of the brain to organise and carry out a sequence of unfamiliar actions (praxis). Motor planning is the first step in learning new skills. Good motor planning ability requires information from all sensory systems of the body. The sensory systems can be described as those from the eyes, ears, skin, muscles, joints and from the movement and gravity receptors provided in the brain. Difficulties may present with:

- Struggling when attempting to master a new skill using unnecessary movement and energy.
- Imitating other children rather than trying to initiate activity themselves as they do not have a strategy.
- Rushing through a task without being able to recognise the different components of the task and realising that they relate to one another. The child may even experience difficulty imitating the actions of others and find it difficult to follow visual instructions.

4. Perception of movement

In order to ensure joint stability, posture, balance, motor control, spatial awareness and a stable visual field, the higher centres of the brain need to receive information about force and gravity. This information is gained from receptors in the inner ear and is known as the vestibular system. The vestibular system also relays information to a part of the brain that regulates attention. Difficulties may present with:

- Mastering and executing rolling, running, hopping, skipping and jumping.
- Using playground equipment such as swings, slides, roundabouts and see-saws.

5. Fine motor control

Fine motor control is the ability to use the hands and fingers precisely for skilled activity. A solid base of good motor and sensory foundation skills is therefore necessary. Without good muscle strength and joint stability in the hands and arms, subconscious awareness of how and where the hands and fingers are moving and adequate tactile sensation and discrimination, it would be difficult to control and use objects of various sizes, weights, shapes and textures. The eye muscles need to work in a coordinated way in order to quickly locate and track objects as well as guide the hand. It is also essential to be able to motor plan, i.e. organise and carry out a sequence of unfamiliar motor tasks and coordinate the two sides of the body. Difficulties may present with:

- Handwriting.
- Using scissors.
- Manipulating small objects.

6. Touch

The tactile system is a dual system incorporating the interpretation of 'protective' and 'discriminative' information. The protective system is responsible for the body automatically withdrawing or defending itself from touch that is interpreted as harmful. The discriminative touch system provides the brain with precise information regarding the properties of objects in the environment. Both systems are essential for tool use and for many aspects of social and emotional development. Difficulties may present with:

- Over- or under-sensitivity to touch, or poor tactile discrimination.
  - Over-sensitive – may be aggressive in interaction with his peers, may avoid art projects especially 'messy play'. There is a need to protect self from unexpected tactile input, and attention difficulties or behaviour difficulties may arise as a result.
  - Under-sensitive – may be unaware of being touched and not react normally to painful experiences such as cuts and bruises.
  - Poor tactile discrimination – problems with grading pressure when manipulating tools and toys.

Development of hand skills in children			
Age	Eyes	Hands	Interrelationship
0-2 months	Random eye movements and vague regard of surroundings	Random and reflexive hand movements	No visual attention to hands
2 months	Attracted by movement periphery; monocular or bi-ocular fixation	Arms activate in response to stimulus; fingers open and close reflexively	Regards hand in ATNR position only with one active eye; releases gaze to surroundings
3 months	Briefly regards own moving hand spontaneously; localises noisy, illuminated moving targets	Swipes and contacts object at side, not mid-line	Watches own hand reach and contact object; alternates or glances from hand to object
	Tracks targets with difficulty through 180°; converges and diverges on targets moving toward and away from self	Sustains grasp on objects placed in hand	Visually searches for object at point of disappearance but cannot combine reach and grasp
	Begins vertical tracking downward losing target	Releases objects involuntarily with awareness after sustained grasp	No retrieval of lost object
4 months	Binocular fixation	Reaches with both hands, contacts and pulls object back against body into mouth	Brings object to mouth without visual monitoring, then relocates after removing
	Prolonged, selective fixation on target in mid-line	Mid-line fingering	Maintains fixation on own hand or object in hand
	Visually pursues lost target outside visual field	Does not reach for lost object	Retrieval not possible when hand and object are not in same visual field
5 months	Shifts gaze (releases fixation) while grasping, manipulating and mouthing target; jerky vertical and diagonal tracking	Reaches with both hands to corral and grasp while shaking object, shoulder/object motion only	No visual attention to hand shaking (manipulating)
	Visually pursues lost target object outside visual field	Hands pursue lost object	Tries to retrieve lost object outside visual field
	Fixates on tiny target (pellet)	No attempt to grasp pellet	Visually attends to pellet but does not approach
6 months	Localises large and small target	Reaches and grasps with one hand	Alternately looks at, mouths, shakes object retaining grasp
	Fixates intensely on pellet	Contacts and rakes pellet	Fixates on pellet while reaching, contacting and raking
	Visually pursues lost target outside visual field unless distracted by another target within visual field	Adjusts body position to reach object outside visual field	Searches for lost object with eyes, hand and body movements
	Shifts gaze in same focal length and with different eyes, different focal lengths	Alternately grasps, mouths, looks, drops, transfers and shakes objects; shoulder and elbow motion	Shifts gaze during adaptive interaction of mouth and hands

Sources: Flavell 1963: McGraw 1969: Erhardt 1982

7. Visual skills

The visual skills required for learning and living can be divided into two groups: physical skills and perceptual skills (see Figure 3.3).

Physical Skills
Convergence
Convergence is the act of directing the eyes inwards towards a near target. The convergence mechanism acts to ensure that both eyes are directed to the same point in space. Failure of this system can lead to double vision, but fatigue and discomfort often linked with attention loss always precedes the failure of the system.

Over-convergence and under-convergence
Both over-convergence and under-convergence can occur. Difficulties may present as:

- Under-convergence – most common, and may be associated with poor concentration, transient doubling of vision at near focus, blurring.
- Over-convergence – reduced working distance as the primary symptom.

Focusing
All classical focusing problems (long-sightedness, short-sightedness and astigmatism) can compromise the individual's ability to produce a clear image when looking at an object. Difficulties in focusing can produce symptoms of fatigue, concentration loss, and (sometimes transient) blurred vision.

Eye movements
Fixation – The ability of the eyes to keep still, and is a prerequisite for any visual task which requires cognition.

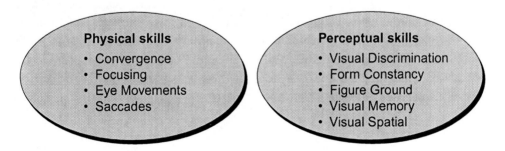

Figure 3.3   Physical skills and perceptual skills

Pursuit – Pursuit movements are those made by the eyes to lock on to and follow or track a moving target through visual space.

Difficulties relating to such eye movement may present as:

- Typically excessive head and/or body movements during reading.
- Problems with handwriting and other hand–eye coordination skills.
- Poor sports performance in ball skills.

Saccades

Saccades occur when a static object is being viewed and the eyes are never static – fixation is never totally stable – tiny jerks of the eyes lasting between 0.1 and 0.3 seconds occur all the time, between which are periods of slight and slow drifts of fixation.

Some children appear to have problems with visual timing, and problems integrating the inward awareness of time with visual input, so that the feedback to the visual control systems results in an increase of the saccadic element of eye movements. This reduces the ability to fixate and to track.

Difficulties may present as:

- Excessive head and/or body movements when reading.
- Use of finger or other pointer to keep place on page.
- Hesitation when changing lines.
- Missing out, jumping over, or rereading words, losing place on the page when looking up at the blackboard.

Perceptual skills

These are the skills required to use visual information to recognise, recall, discriminate and make meaning of what we see.

Development

As a child develops he or she begins to explore the world with eyes and hands to form mental connections about how things look and feel. Through touch, movement and vision, the child learns. However in order to develop perceptual skills, the child requires good visual attention. As the child's ability to conceptualise and think about what they see expands, so does their visual attention. Three components of visual attention that affect learning are:

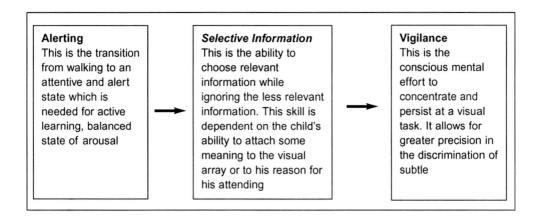

Alerting	Selective Information	Vigilance
This is the transition from walking to an attentive and alert state which is needed for active learning, balanced state of arousal	This is the ability to choose relevant information while ignoring the less relevant information. This skill is dependent on the child's ability to attach some meaning to the visual array or to his reason for his attending	This is the conscious mental effort to concentrate and persist at a visual task. It allows for greater precision in the discrimination of subtle

Visual discrimination

Visual discrimination is the ability to detect the similarities and differences in shape, form, colour, pattern, size, sequential order and orientation. Development of skills in this area produces opportunities to promote language, i.e. classification. Discrimination abilities appear first and seem to provide the foundation upon which the other abilities are built. The following elements in visual discrimination are important:

Form Perception
Is the ability to *recognise, match*, and *name* objects, shapes, patterns, or symbols by the *essential details*. It also involves the ability to appreciate that a basic shape or item, e.g. 3 or 2 dimensions remain constant, i.e. form constancy, even though it may vary in size or colour. It appears that babies possess a crude ability to recognise and respond to colour, shapes and patterns. Constancy develops by about seven years of age and is mature by about 11 years of age.

Visual Closure or Whole/Part Relationships
Is required in order to understand the relationship of the 'whole' to its 'parts' in visual discrimination. It requires not only the ability to recognise whole forms but also to become more aware of spatial organisation and relationship between components.

Figure Ground
Is the ability to extract and distinguish individual items from the background in which they are embedded. Good visual attention is required

Children who have problems with visual discrimination may present with the following:

- Difficulty in matching shapes, symbols, letters, numerals and words.
- Difficulty in recognising differences in numerals, letters, shapes, words and objects.
- Exhibit reversals and inversions in writing letters and numbers.
- Forget to punctuate or make odd punctuation marks.
- Use capital letters in the middle of a sentence.
- Be disorganised and inattentive.
- Cannot put parts together to form a whole shape.
- Difficulty blending letters into words visually.
- Unable to identify indistinct representation of familiar objects.
- Difficulty shifting attention appropriately.
- Difficulty scanning and therefore skip sections of work.
- Lose place when reading, writing or copying.
- Difficulty completing work on 'busy' paper.
- Difficulty recognising that two- and three-dimensional forms belong to certain categories, whatever their size, colour, texture, mode of representation or the angle from which they are seen.
- Difficulties in reading and writing as may be unable to recognise the same letters or words or numbers presented in a different manner, i.e. different colour, size or text.

Visual memory

Visual memory is a combination of different types of memory:

- Short-term memory – needed for activities such as immediate recall of displayed material, and for the reproduction of shapes, forms or symbols, and the recall of recent visual experiences.
- Long-term memory – concerned with retrieving visual images which are appropriate and relevant to new learning situations.
- Sequential memory – an integral part of visual decoding when reading and encoding when spelling.

The development of efficient visual memory is dependent upon:

- attention and concentration;
- keen observation;
- speed;
- good motivation.

Its relationship to other forms of memory (movement, hearing and touch) should also be remembered, particularly with children who appear to have poor memories. The role of language in labelling and fixing visual experience and in the development of visualisation and visual imagery is also of fundamental importance.

Children who have difficulties with visual memory may:

- Be unable to remember non-verbal experiences.
- Be able to reproduce a given structure/symbol from a model, but be unable to reproduce it when the model is removed.
- Mis-spell a word several different ways on the same paper.
- Be able to remember all letters in a word, but get them in the wrong sequence.
- Have difficulty in left to right progression.
- Make mistakes when copying work from the board.

Visual-spatial perception

Visual-spatial perception is how a person perceives the relationship of external space to his body as well as objects in space relative to other objects.

Locomotion provides the child with experience to learn about the relationship between him or herself and the physical environment. As the child explores the space around them, their sense of movement, body awareness and visual input comes together to form an internal map of the relationship between themselves, objects and space. Initially, visual-spatial perception develops as the child moves over, under, around and through objects in the course of their play. As these experiences are organised in the brain, perceptual skills such as form constancy, position of objects in space, figure ground and depth perception begin to emerge. The ability to place cognitive labels on space such as right, left, above and below requires that these perceptual foundations be well established physically.

Visual-spatial perception provides us with information about our environment. Children who have difficulties with visual-spatial perception may:

- have difficulty getting from one place to another without getting lost;
- have inadequate judgement of distance and height;
- bump into things; knock over objects, e.g. spilling drink;
- may have difficulty executing stairs and kerbs, pouring from containers;
- be disorganised;
- have difficulties in knowing where to start writing on paper;
- have difficulties catching a ball or hitting with a bat/racquet;
- find shooting at targets difficult;
- produce letters which vary in size, spacing and alignment;
- have poor letter and number recognition; reversal of letters can be a common problem;

- have difficulty copying from the blackboard;
- have difficulty staying within personal boundaries.

> **Discussion** – What other 'conditions' may present if there is an absence or delay in acquisition of the fundamental sensory motor skills?

8. Language processing

What is language?

Language is used for communication, most of which involves interactions with other people. As people interact in different circumstances, they need to use language in order to maintain contact with others, gain information, give information and accomplish goals. People do not just talk: they do things with words and sentences. Language therefore consists of different ways in which speakers vary what they say according to the needs of different listeners in different circumstances, i.e. using alternative ways of saying the same thing to achieve the same purpose. For example it is possible to get a drink of water by:

- Asking a question – 'Do you have any water?'
- Making a statement – 'I am thirsty.'
- Referring to it by name – 'Here comes the water.'
- Using a pronoun – 'Here it comes!'

Language is a code and is a means of representation of ideas about the world. It is a system in which sounds combine to form words and words combine to form sentences for representing knowledge, and is determined by a system of rules. Noam Chomsky (1972) stated:

> Having mastered a language, one is able to understand an indefinite number of expressions that are new to one's experience . . . and one is able, with greater or less facility, to produce such expressions on an appropriate occasion, despite their novelty and independently of detectable stimulus configurations, and to be understood by others who share this still mysterious ability. The normal use of language is, in this sense, a creative activity. . . . A person who knows a language has mastered a system of rules that assigns sound and meaning in a definite way for an infinite class of possible sentences. . . . Of course, the person who knows the language has no consciousness of having mastered these rules or of putting them to use, nor is there any reason to suppose that this knowledge of the rules of language can be brought to consciousness.

The ability to decide what form the message should take depends on the ability to make inferences about what the listener already knows and needs to know, and how well the speaker knows the listener, as well as the status between speaker and listener. Therefore in addition to learning about the world from the content of language, and learning the linguistic code for the form representing language content, it is also necessary to learn how to recognise different kinds of circumstances that require different kinds of language use.

It is possible to identify three major components of language:

- Content – topic – an idea encoded in a message, and categorisations of topics – general objects, actions or possessions.

  The development of children's language *content* depends on the interaction between their knowledge (the information about objects and events in the world that is represented in memory) and the context (the persons, objects and events that surround the children). The interaction between knowledge and context is *information processing*, whereby like events are related and generalisations are formed to be represented in memory. Thus, the content of language is its meaning or *semantics*.
- Form – acoustics and phonetic shape. Form can be described in several ways: units of sound, *phonology*; units of meaning (words or inflections), *morphology*; units of meaning combined with one another, *syntax*.
- The use of language – this is considered in two ways: the reasons why people speak, and how individuals understand and choose forms of language. Language use consists of the socially and cognitively determined selection of behaviours according to the goals of the speaker and the context of the situation. The social use of language in particular is discussed in later chapters.

Early communication

Although a child is communicating from the moment of their first cry, their vocalising is not purposeful but reflexive, reflecting feelings of discomfort, hunger or pleasure. Communication with intention develops as the child becomes aware that their behaviour has an effect upon their environment. This relationship is assisted by the carer's responsiveness to the behaviour.

Although early vocalisations are reflexive, carers give meaning to them and respond accordingly, e.g. the child smiles and the carer smiles back. This communication increases as the child is able to take a more active part and requires the following requisites:

- attention;
- co-actions – activities which child and carers engage in simultaneously; mutual feedback is necessary to maintain interaction;
- alternate actions – alternate exchanges, i.e. imitation.

Early vocalisation

From an early age children learn to use vocalisation in many ways. Haliday (1973) identifies the following functions:

- Interactional – from 3–4 months of age to maintain social exchanges.
- Personal – from 9 months to express feelings and states.
- Instrumental – from 10½ months to satisfy needs and desires.
- Regulatory – from 10½ months to control actions of specific people.
- Heuristic – approximately 15 months to obtain information.
- Informative – approximately 18 months to give information.
- Imaginative – 18 months to play and create.
- Dialogue – approximately 2 years to maintain social communication.

Early concepts

As the infant grows and develops its early learning is dominated by the acquisition of *concepts*, i.e. information about the properties and functions of objects and also how these relate to one another. The main components are:

- Object concept
  - constancy
  - permanence
  - identity
- Relational concept – Children learn about this by looking, listening and doing. Movement change is a dominant force in their development where children learn to identify which objects move by themselves and which need to be propelled.
- Cause and effect – Through the repetition of 'accidental' activities, the developing child soon learns that their movements have an effect and they begin to learn to separate him or herself from the environment. The child therefore begins to coordinate information from the senses. Within the context of language the child will begin to learn to seek causes and reasons for why things are as they are, and to work through problems by anticipating the effect one action has upon another.
- Speech perception – In order to comprehend verbal language a developing child must learn to be able to:
  - discriminate the human voice from environmental sounds
  - discriminate speech from other human sounds
  - discriminate differences between speech sounds.

Early verbal understanding

Symbolic understanding develops gradually from 9 to 27 months and is consistent in its stages:

- Situational understanding – gained from experiences of the environment;
- Symbolic understanding – showing awareness of symbolic representation, i.e. meaningful play with toys.

Summary of speech and language development			
Approximate age	Verbal comprehension and auditory response	Expressive language	Vocalisation C: consonant V: vowel
0–6 weeks	• Startles • Quiets to voice • Child attends mainly to own body and its movements	• Communication is reflexive and not intentional • Meaning is imposed by parent/carers • Smiles, 4–6 weeks	• Differentiated cries and vegetative sounds • Vowel sounds appear

3 months	• Turns to source of voice
	• Child can attend to objects and events in the environment as directed by adult
		• 'Co-actions':
		  – mutual gaze
		  – sustained eye contact
		  – synchronised head movements and co-vocalisations
			• First consonants heard from 12–24 weeks. Early consonants are p/b and k/g
			• From 16 weeks emergence of babbling. Frequency and intensity of vocalisations are influenced by whether or not child is comfortable, stimulated or gets a response

6 months	• Responds to emotional tones of mother's voice	• 'Alternate actions' (turn-taking) takes over from Co-action • Co-actions predominate during times of excitement • Parents beginning to impute different intentions to vocalisations	• Reduplicate babbling: (CVCV sequence with unchanging consonant) e.g. 'dudada'. Sounds may include: p,b,m,n,w,d,k,g • May use non-English sounds
9 months	• Object permanence • Situational understanding, e.g. understands simple requests with clues from gesture and routine • Responds to own name (10 months) • Understands 'no' and 'bye-bye'	• Communication is intentional • Vocalises deliberately as means of interpersonal communication • Protoimperative (use of adult to obtain object) and protodeclarative (use of object to attain joint attention with adult)	• Imitates sounds jargon (babble with rise–fall intonation) • Non-reduplicated babble occurs and may persist until 18 months (CVC or VCV sequence: consonant may differ from one syllable to the next)
1 year	• Understands many familiar words and simple commands associated with gestures, e.g. 'come to daddy' • Spontaneous definition by use of common objects applied to self • Symbolic play with large toys (15 months)	• Speaks 2–6 real words • Spontaneous use of single words in correct context; mostly used to request actions or objects or refer (call attention) to things in the environment • Continuous tuneful 'conversation-like' jargon	• Most vowel sounds heard by this stage. First words often embedded in strings of jargon and are often reduplicated syllables, e.g. 'dada' • Vocalises and moves to familiar songs • Child now begins to relearn sounds that he/she has babbled as meaningful (phonemic) contrasts

18 months	• Knows some face/body parts on self/doll
	• Will find objects on request
	• Follows instructions, e.g. 'Come here' and 'Stop that'
	• Symbolic play with miniature toys
		• 6–20+ words
		• Attempts to sing
		• Imitates prominent words in sentence addressed to him/her
		• Some two- or three-word sentences: function is mostly 'request' or 'reference' and word order is correct. Refers to self and others by name; some pronouns
			• Phonemes acquired: m,n,p,b,t,d,w
			• Phonological processes include:
			  – reduplication
			  – consonant deletion
			  – cluster reduction
			  – fronting
			  – stopping
			  – gliding (/r/ → [w]
			  – context sensitive voicing

2 years	• Follows instructions involving two verbal concepts (which are nouns), e.g. 'Put the *cup* in the box' • Can match object or toy to picture	• May use about 200 words • Uses two- and three-word sentences – mainly nouns • Asks questions: 'What?', 'Where?' • Joins in songs and rhymes	• New phonemes: 'ng', 'k', 'g', 'h', final consonant deletion, cluster reduction, some fronting, stopping gliding and context sensitive voicing are present
2½ years	• Understands first verbs • Understands instructions, involving up to three concepts, e.g. 'Put the *big dolly* on the *chair*' • Knows big/small, on/under • Understands pronouns • Plays out sequences with small toys, e.g. tea party • Can match pictures to a multi-object picture	• Begins to use more verbs in sentences of four or more words • Uses 200 or more recognisable words • Most common question: 'What?' • Uses pronouns 'I', 'Me', 'You' • Learns grammatical morphemes: -ing, plural-s, past tense -ed, etc. • Stammering in eagerness is common	• New phonemes: f,s,j,l • Final consonant deletion, cluster reduction, stopping, fronting of /sh/ → [s], gliding and some context sensitive voicing are present

3 years	• Most pronouns used appropriately
	• Knows several colours
		• Child expands subject and object of sentence: '*Big train* gone now', 'He lost *his* shoe'
		• Most common questions:
		  – 'Where?'
		  – 'Who?'
		  – Use of 'and'
		• Directs actions in play out loud: 'That goes there'
		• Begins to use verb auxiliaries
			• Consonant clusters appear, e.g. 'pl', 'cl', 'sp', 'st'...
			• Stopping, fronting /sh/→[s] and gliding present
			• New phonemes at 3½ years: 'v', 'z', 'sh', 'ch', 'dg', 'r'

4 years	• Knows most colours • Begins to learn abstract concepts: hard, soft, rough, smooth (4½ years) • Language used for reasoning	• Grammar correct for the most part • Most common question: 'Why?' • Tag questions appear, e.g. 'Didn't I?'	• Speech fully intelligible • Most clusters are established • Some immaturities: usually th/f, r/w, ch/dg and some clusters • Gliding present • New phoneme at 4½ years: 'th'

> **Discussion** – What factors could influence the acquisition of sensory motor skills?

Stages of play		
Age	**Stage**	**Type of play**
0–2 years	Sensory – motor	• Repetition • Self-centred • Trial and error • Solitary play
2–4 years	Symbolic and simple construction	• Social interaction • Pretend – imaginative • Organises • Takes pride – 'look what I have done'
4–7 years	Dramatic, complex constructive, pre-game stage	• Widening social participation – seeks companionship and may have imaginary friends • Role playing • Daredevil • Intention precedes action
7–12 years	Game stage	• Social interaction with same sex • Competition – sport • Clubs • Imaginative play – costumes

> **Discussion** – What difficulties might a child with DCD have in accessing play activities? How might this affect him or her at home, school and in the community?

References

Chomsky, N. (1972) *Language and Mind.* New York: Harcourt Brace.

Cratty, B. J. (1970) *Perceptual Motor Development in Infants and Children.* London: Macmillan.

Erhardt, R. P. (1994) *Developmental Hand Dysfunction: Theory, Assessment, and Treatment,* 2nd edn. San Antonio, TX: Therapy Skill Builders, a Division of The Psychological Corporation.

Frostig, M., Lefever, W. and Whittsley, J. R. B. (1966) *Marianne Frostig Developmental Test of Visual Perception.*

Haliday, M. A. K. (1973) *Explorations in the Functions of Language.* (In the series Explorations in Language Study: General editors, P. Doughty and G. Thornton.) London: Edward Arnold.

Keogh, I. F. Jr. and Sugden, D. (1985) *Movement Skill Development.* New York: Macmillan.

Wilson, R. A. (1998) *Special Educational Needs in the Early Years.* London: Routledge.

CHAPTER 4

Assessing the child with DCD

Learning objectives
- To examine the characteristics of assessment.
- To reflect upon assessment instruments that may be used with individuals with DCD.
- To consider methods of planning for intervention.

Learning outcomes
- To be able to apply evaluation techniques according to role and setting.
- To be able to construct specific goals, aims and objectives when establishing individualised and targeted learning plans.

Introduction

The increasing awareness and interest in DCD raises many issues for those professionals receiving referrals for assessment and treatment. However, the acknowledged coexisting features with which the children often present can be misleading in terms of to whom the initial referral should be made.

The identification of DCD requires a comprehensive assessment that includes a reliable and valid assessment of the child's motor skills. In addition, assessment needs to include observations of how the child interacts with his or her environment, as well as the quality of their movements. Missiuna and Pollock (1995) demonstrated the importance of clinical observation and teacher report in the identification of children with motor problems and recommended that therapists evaluate the consistency of data obtained from standardised tests, clinical observations and historical and anecdotal information.

Careful evaluation of multiple sources of information is especially important in the field of DCD because there is no 'gold standard'; no one test or screening measure that can be used alone to confidently identify the problem (Crawford *et al.* 2001).

Identification of children with DCD or assignment of diagnostic terms like 'awkwardness' have been based largely on normed referenced tests with no measure of the intelligence that motor incoordination might have on activities of daily living (Bouffard *et al.* 1996, Causgrove and Watkinson 1994, Dwyer and McKenzie 1994, Schoemaker and Kalverboer 1994). This implies an assumption that both criteria A and B (see DSM IV criteria in Chapter 1) can be assessed simultaneously. However, this assumption has not been formally tested.

Assessment should therefore include the most commonly used tasks within the relevant context. Burton and Davis (1996), Davis and van Emmerik (1995) and Davis and Burton (1991), suggest that the performance of a movement skill is a product of the task, the environment and the performer.

Why assess?

- What is the purpose of assessment?
- Is there a functional problem that is stopping the individual accessing activities of daily living, the curriculum or gaining a place in employment?
- How severe is the problem?
- What is the nature of the deficit?
- How will the assessment help the individual in accessing help/remediation or knowing where else to refer for further help?

Issues surrounding assessment

Prevalence
One of the difficulties in the assessment of individuals with DCD is the variability in the reported incidence. Depending on the assessment procedure and the background and experience of the assessor, the incidence can range from 6 to 22 per cent (Cermak 2002, Kadesjo and Gilberg 1999, Revie and Larkin 1993, Maeland 1992, Keogh *et al.* 1979, Gubbay 1975).

Available resources
The impact of this prevalence on both the Health and Education services should those individuals be referred is staggering. Already there are waiting lists across the UK for assessment and treatment and the situation is further compounded by the increasing shortage of both professionals allied to medicine (Occupational Therapists, Physiotherapists and Speech and Language Therapists) and specialised teaching staff. Naturally, this is a cause of great concern for all involved, parent,

teacher and therapist, giving rise to a sense of great frustration and helplessness in their ability to enable the children 'before it's too late'. In response to this, many organisations are taking it upon themselves to offer services. There are many issues regarding this and some causes of concern, for example the use of unqualified or poorly/inappropriately trained personnel, alternative and unresearched approaches being implemented. This aspect is discussed further in Chapter 10.

Priority
In light of resource deficits, many services within the UK do not consider children with DCD as a priority, and yet research has demonstrated that motor problems in children can be very distressing and have significant long-term consequences. Studies have found that children with DCD display poor social competency, have more academic and behaviour problems, and have low self-esteem (Cantell *et al.* 1994, Geuze and Borger 1993, Losse *et al.* 1991). Many consider that these children do not have a disability, and yet if this condition is considered within the model evolved by the World Health Organisation, it can be seen that these individuals clearly fit the criteria.

- Impairment – is the loss or abnormality of psychological or anatomical function.
- Disability – is any restriction or lack of ability to perform an activity in the manner or within the range considered normal for a human being.
- Handicap – is a disadvantage for a given individual, resulting from an impairment or disability, that limits or prevents the fulfilment of a role that is normal (depending on age, sex or culture) for that individual.

Roles and responsibilities
In view of the coexisting and complex presentation of individuals with DCD, whose job is it to assess/screen?

Paediatrician	Educational Psychologist	Occupational Therapist
Parent	Child	Teacher
Physiotherapist	Speech and Language Therapist	SENCO

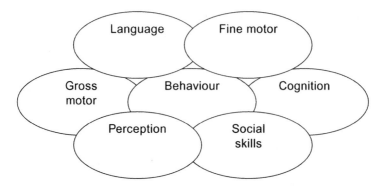

Figure 4.1   Coexistence of features

In view of the coexisting features of individuals with DCD, it would be reasonable to suggest that no one professional should assess and subsequently diagnose in isolation.

> **Discussion** – How could information be exchanged effectively between different organisations such as Health and Education? What are the limitations of working in isolation and what can be gained from working collaboratively? How could services be developed to accommodate resource deficits?

Information gathering

Assessment and screening

An assessment should be carried out in a systematic way. For an assessment to be valid it should also involve more than one tool and strategy. It is important to gather information which samples performance in a variety of ways and settings.

Assessment is a very important aspect of evaluating an individual's strengths and needs. However, there are a number of ways to measure skills:

- Performance outcome – this refers to an outcome or result of performing a skill (distance, time).
- Performance production – this refers to specific aspects in the execution of the task (slow, fast, force).

In order that appropriate decisions can be made about intervention, placement, programme planning and performance objectives for children with motor impairments, it is critical that appropriate assessment methods and accurate screening tests are used (Zittle 1994).

> Assessment enables the examiner to evaluate current skills, changes, delays, and gain an insight into learning and teaching strategies.

Screening should identify children who are at risk for developing various learning or behaviour problems (Gredler 1997, 1992). Screening results can indicate a *possible cause* for concern, but cannot be used to confirm a specific diagnosis. Screening procedures are also not appropriate for planning programmes of intervention, nor should they be used for grouping children for remediation purposes. Some screening procedures focus on the developmental status of the child; others on physical and health concerns and/or sensory functioning.

Some investigators use a two-step process to identify children who are suspected of having DCD. This is an initial screen to identify a cohort that then requires further in-depth testing.

The two-step process usually includes:

(a) An initial screening for indicators of motor competence.
(b) Followed by a confirmatory motor test (Smyth and Mason 1998, Volman and Geuze 1998, Van der Meulen *et al.* 1991, Geuze and Kalverboer 1987).

Typical procedures have involved any of the following:

- The teacher's or parents' identification of a child as one whose motor performance falls below that expected of children of the same age (Murphy and Gliner 1998).
- Whose motor development lags behind intellectual development (Laslow *et al.* 1988).
- Whose motor behaviour appears clumsy (Volman and Geuze 1998).

These indicators are not necessarily markers of interference of activities of daily living (ADL) but rather predictors of motor incoordination.

One of the most popular measures, especially used in North America and particularly by therapists, is the Bruininks-Oseretsky Test of Motor Proficiency. An alternative test frequently used outside of the United States and Canada is the Movement ABC Battery for Children (Henderson and Sugden 1992). This includes an observational checklist of movement skills within the context of daily living, as well as items assessing behaviour problems which might interfere with movement performance.

Parent reports as a source of information on children's current skills and deficits have been found to be quite sensitive, reliable, and valid (Faraone *et al.* 1995,

Glascoe and Dworkin 1995). They can provide a qualitative and accurate assessment of the child's skills in daily life which encompasses the principles of family-centred care (Pollock and Stewart 1998). The Developmental Coordination Disorder Questionnaire (DCDQ) is a newly developed measure that assesses parents' perceptions of their children's motor skills. However, no additional studies have been completed at this present time. Parent report methods such as the DCDQ have a number of advantages compared with standardised tests. Firstly they are less time-consuming; also they are less expensive, and allow for the investigations of children's daily living skills.

Assessment of interference with activities of daily living (ADL) requires the delineation of specific relevant activities. One of the most common daily experiences of children is their play. However, children's behaviour and performance may be subject to where and with whom they are working. Performance, therefore, varies across a variety of settings.

In a study by Crawford, Wilson and Dewey (2001) comparing the Bruininks-Oseretsky Test of Motor Proficiency, the Movement ABC Battery for Children and the Developmental Coordination Disorder Questionnaire, the researchers concluded that the measures did not consistently identify children as DCD or non-DCD. However, their findings suggested that information from standardised tests, combined together with a picture of the child's functional performance, may increase the likelihood that DCD will be accurately identified. They further stated that judgement-based assessment and observation are necessary to augment standardised tests and to confirm the presence of a motor problem. No one test therefore can accurately identify DCD children or replace clinical reasoning of a therapist who examines multiple sources of information about a child's functional skills.

Discussion – What information should be gathered prior to the assessment? Who should collect this information and how would it be best related to those individuals involved?

Key characteristics of an assessment instrument

The key characteristics of an assessment instrument are that it should have:

- Reliability – a test that is reliable will provide consistent scores from one test administration to another.
- Validity – a condition when a test measures what it claims to measure.
- Objectivity.

Assessment tools can be *categorised* in various ways:

- Normed referenced tests – these are based on statistical sampling of hundreds or even thousands of individuals. They permit the comparison of an individual against a statistical sample that is intended to be representative of the population at large.
- Criterion referenced tests – assessment instruments that incorporate a pre-established standard to which the individual's score is compared.
- Standardised tests – have set procedures for administration and scoring. These provide precise measurements of an individual's performance in specific areas and usually describe this performance as a standard score (Case-Smith 2001). There seems to be no doubt about the usefulness of standardised tools compared with non-standardised tools in providing objective effectiveness (De Clive-Lowe 1996). However, measures must be chosen appropriately and be suitable in line with the purpose for which they were developed (Ovretveit 1998).

Discussion – What considerations should be given when selecting assessment tools? How does the issue of co-morbidity of DCD with other conditions cause confusion and difficulty when establishing a label, and choosing appropriate assessment tools and the professionals who administer them?

Tools available
The following are some of the tests available and more generally used by health professionals. They are not all diagnostic, some being screening tools.

Children's assessments
- Denver Developmental Screening Test (Frankenburg and Dodds 1967 and Frankenburg *et al.* 1990). This is the most widely used standardised test for evaluating motor development in young children, incorporating gross and fine motor skills, language and personal social skills. Designed for children two weeks to six years of age.
- Bayley Scales of Infant Development (Bayley 1969). This test considers mental, motor and behaviour. It has been most extensively researched and is considered one of the best behavioural techniques available for infants. Designed for children from one month to two-plus years.
- Peabody Developmental Motor Scales. This test is designed to assess fine and gross motor skills of children from birth to 6.9 years of age.
- Schedule of Growing Skills II (Bellman *et al.* 1996). A developmental

screening procedure based on the work by Dr Mary Sheridan. Designed to be used as part of child health surveillance programmes for children 0–60 months.

- Purdue Perceptual Motor Survey (Roach and Kephart 1966). This is not considered to be a true test but more a behavioural assessment survey. Designed for children of six to ten years, it has been used to successfully discriminate between children who experience difficulties in motor develop-ment. Interpretations and generalisations are therefore limited.

- Bruininks-Oseretsky Test of Motor Proficiency (Bruininks 1978). This test assesses the motor function of children from four-plus to 14-plus.

- Fundamental Movement Pattern Assessment Instrument (McClenaghan 1976, McClenaghan and Gallahue 1978 and Gallahue and Ozmun 1995). This is an observational assessment instrument designed to classify an indi-vidual at the 'initial', 'elementary' or 'mature' stage of development. It is a subjective test designed to evaluate the present status of children and to assess change over time. It views children's quality of movement. It cannot be used for comparing one child against another as it does not yield a quantitative score.

- Developmental Sequence of Fundamental Motor Skills Inventory (Seefeldt and Haubenstricker 1976 and Haubenstricker 1981). This test categorises ten fundamental motor patterns into four/five stages.

- Test of Gross Motor Development (Ulrich 1985). This test assesses selective movement skills in children three to ten years and takes into account loco-motor and manipulative skills.

- Ohio State University Scale of Intra-Gross Motor Assessment. Developed to measure basic locomotor and manipulative skills in children 2.5 years to 14 years.

- Basic Motor Ability Tests – Revised (Arnheim and Sinclair 1979). Designed to assess a variety of motor functions including gross and fine motor control, eye/hand coordination, motor control, agility and joint flexibility. Can be used on a group of children.

- Movement ABC Battery for Children (Henderson and Sugden 1992). Designed for children four to 12 years. The test takes into account ball skills, static and dynamic balance and manual dexterity.

- Pediatric Evaluation of Disability Inventory (PEDI) (Hayley *et al.* 1992). Developed as a standardised tool to identify and measure function in children six months to seven years six months.

- The School Function Assessment (Coster *et al.* 1998). A criterion referenced tool for children five to 12 years. It examines the child's pattern of participa-tion in school activities and environments that are typical of peers in the same context.

- Ecological Task Analysis. This is an approach to examining performance in light of the relationships between the task goal, the environment and the performer.

Adult assessments

There are some adult assessment tools available but there are no specific assessment tools that will diagnose DCD in the adult.

- American Alliance for Health, Physical Education, Recreation and Dance Field Test for Older Adults. This test measures a combination of health-related physical fitness components and motor performance characteristics. Test items are designed to relate to daily functions.
- Scales of Activities of Daily Living (Law and Letts 1989).
- Williams-Greene Test of Physical Motor Function. Designed to measure the upper extremity function and mobility capabilities of older adults.
- The Assessment of Motor and Process Skills (AMPS) (Fisher 1999).

> **Discussion** – What are the limitations and considerations in assessing adults compared to children?

Language assessments

- Clinical Evaluation of Language Fundamentals (CELF) – 3. This looks at receptive and expressive language. The following subtests are included:
  - Sentence structure
  - Word structure
  - Concepts and directions
  - Formulated sentences
  - Word classes
  - Recalling sentences
  - Sentence assembly
  - Semantic relationships
  - Word associations
  - Listening to paragraphs
  - Rapid automatic naming
- The Test of Pragmatic Language (TOPL). An individually administered instrument designed to assess pragmatic language skills that can be used with students in kindergarten through to high school. It is more specifically intended for use with children, adolescents, and adults with learning disabilities, language delays, reading difficulties, or aphasia. It is said to provide

information on six dimensions of pragmatic language: physical setting, audience, topic, purpose, visual–gestural cues, and abstraction.

- The Children's Communication Checklist (CCC). Developed to provide an objective assessment of pragmatic aspects of children's communication difficulties.
- The Listening Skills Test. The test is in four parts and assesses the ability to make judgements about the efficacy of verbal messages or instructions. Tasks include relating messages to arrays of pictorial items, making judgements about statements that refer to one complex picture, marking routes on a street plan in response to an extended set of instructions, and the ability to evaluate purely verbal utterances. The overall aim of the test is to assess children's ability to make sense on their own of verbal information in a decontextualised situation thought to represent the nature of much transactional communication in the classroom.
- Test of Adolescent and Adult Language, (3rd edn) (TOAL – 3). Determines strengths and weaknesses across the language domain, including:
  - Listening – the ability to understand the spoken language of other people.
  - Speaking – the ability to express one's ideas orally.
  - Reading – the ability to comprehend written messages.
  - Writing – the ability to express thoughts in graphic form.
  - Spoken language – the ability to listen and speak.
  - Written language – the ability to read and write vocabulary; the ability to understand and use words in communication.
  - Grammar – the ability to understand and generate syntactic (and morphological) structures.
  - Receptive language – the ability to comprehend both written and spoken language.
  - Expressive language – the ability to produce written and spoken language.

Assessing non-verbal skills

- Informal methods
  - Television – Choose an appropriate programme showing substantial interactions between children and adults (Sesame Street, daytime soaps), turn off the sound and ask the child to tell you what is going on by simply watching the picture. Every so often turn up the volume to determine the child's accuracy. Focus on different types of non-verbal communication separately and in combination with each other: what do the characters' facial expressions indicate? How about when the facial expressions are combined with postures? Conversely the child could turn away from the screen and listen only to the sound while trying to describe what he or she thinks is going on visually. If the characters are shouting, what should their

facial expressions indicate? What posture might a whispering character take?

o Observe – The child observes people interacting in various places and ask the child to say what he or she thinks is going on or what if any relationships these people might share. People-watching can provide a wealth of social exchanges to discuss. Observe the child interact with others at parties, in arguments, while watching sports events, a movie, or TV. Through these observations gain an awareness of how easily others might misinterpret how the child is feeling. If this is difficult for the trained observer, the chances are that others will have difficulty as well.

o Photographs or a video recorder – These can be more systematic for observations. Ask the child to show certain emotions and record his or her attempts. But remember this technique is reactive, as the child is reacting to performing.

Cognitive assessment

• Wechsler Pre-School and Primary Scale of Intelligence (WIPSI) and Wechsler Intelligence Scale for Children (WISC) (6 years to 16.11 years). These tests give a comprehensive profile of non-verbal and verbal skills.

Verbal scores	Performance scores (non-verbal)
Information	Picture completion
Similarities	Coding
Arithmetic	Picture arrangement
Vocabulary	Block design
Comprehension	Object assembly
Digit span	Symbol search
	Mazes

Other methods of information gathering
• Parent interviews
• Parent questionnaires
• Teacher interviews
• Teacher questionnaires
• Child-centred questionnaires
• Work samples
• Systematic observations
• Information from other professionals such as previous reports
• Video
• Stills photography

> **Discussion** – How can the parent and the child be more integral to the assessment process?

Planning for intervention

In order to provide effective intervention for children with DCD individualised programmes need to be established. The framework for this is centred around the assessment findings. It is important that the assessment findings do not relate only to scores or developmental age, but also to what the child could do and how he or she learns best. Considerations are as follows:

- What can the child do, i.e. what is the child's current level of skill?
- What skills are in the process of being acquired?
- What critical skills must the child attain?
- What seems to work?
- What would the child like to improve?
- What are the concerns of the parents?
- How can the programme be implemented in an integrated fashion, i.e. embedded in the context of broader curriculum delivery?

Setting goals and measuring change

Establishing goals, aims and objectives

We need to establish goals, aims and objectives because they:

- provide direction;
- provide guidelines for evaluation;
- convey instructional intent to others.

Goals, aims and objectives are not the same things.

- A *goal* usually represents a more long-term plan for achievement. It usually identifies the general area to be addressed. It serves as the general heading for the more specific aims and objectives, e.g. for John to be able to participate independently in PE activities.
- An *aim* normally consists of a statement of general intent and is more short term in nature. It may use an item or example to represent the final approvable behaviour of the participant at the conclusion of the task/session/ programme.

- By contrast, an *objective* states the requirements in precise terms.

Examples of the above are:

- Long-term goal: Thomas will be able to participate independently in ball skills activities during PE sessions.
- Short-term aim (there may need to be more than one aim to achieve the above): By the end of six sessions, Thomas will be able to catch a football with two hands successfully from two metres while in a standing position.
- Objectives (how we are going to achieve the aim): During PE sessions, on a weekly basis, Thomas will successfully pass a beach ball to and fro with another player while sat on the floor in a stable position ten out of ten times.

Often the easiest thing is to be able to establish the long-term goal. It is somewhat harder to set the shorter-term aims. However, the hardest part is establishing the objectives, because this is where knowledge of the activity and skill base of the child is fundamental. Often targets are set for an individual and not realised; this is because the challenge is set too high and not reviewed in order to assess the achievement.

Principles of planning

The following principles should apply to planning:

- Set the goals
- Ensure good planning (objectives)
- Do the task
- Check the outcome

If there is failure, it is rarely down to the child, but to the aims and objectives set in the first place which are not adequate to meet their needs. In these instances, revise the plan and start again.

Goals, aims and objectives must be realistic and achievable within the constraints placed upon the individuals involved, whether they relate to time, resources, facilities or any other factor which is likely to affect outcome.

How to write objectives

All objectives should be stated in terms of observable behaviour or performance and should not merely describe what the individual has learnt or become familiar with in the time allocated for the programme. An objective should also be measurable in some form so that it can be tested. For example:

By the end of the session the child will be able to:

.... (an action word – something observable)

.... (item – normally an object)

.... (condition – describes the variables)

.... (standard – the measurable criteria)

An example of the above is:

Thomas will be able to catch (Action) the ball (Item) from 2 metres (Condition) ten out of ten times (Standard).

Other aspects to be considered when planning for intervention are:

- What is the focus of learning? The objective may be cross-curricular or pertinent to one area of learning/function.
- What is the target group? The activity may be designed to meet individual or group needs.
- What is the individual's prior learning?
- What is the ability to extend activities?
- Are there any further opportunities for assessment?
- What are the long-term targets for the future?

Discussion – What are the difficulties in implementing individualised and targeted programmes for individuals with DCD?

Recording outcome

It is necessary to record outcome to:

- Check the standard;
- Measure performance against goals set;
- Ensure best practice;
- Implement change;
- Identify the need for further remediation.

The following tools can be used:

- objective versus subjective testing

- quantitative versus qualitative testing (comparisons)
- observation
- self-evaluation
- rating scales

Recording systems

When implementing a system it is important to take into account the following:

- targets to be achieved
- teaching strategies to be used
- provision to be put in place
- review date
- outcome of any action taken

An example of an Individualised Education Plan is provided here. This is followed by seven further examples of recording outcome. (These seven examples are followed by a Discussion question.)

Example of an Individualised Education Plan					
Name:_____ Areas of concern:_____ Class teacher:_____ Support by:_____ Proposed support:_____ Start date:_____			Stage: 2 Year group/IEP No.:_ Review date:_____ Support began:_____		
Targets to be achieved	**Achievement criteria**	**Possible resources/ techniques**	**Possible class strategies**	**Ideas for support/ assistant**	**Outcome**
1.	1.	1.	1.	1.	1.
2.	2.	2.	2.	2.	2.
3.	3.	3.	3.	3.	3.
4.	4.	4.	4.	4.	4.
5.	5.	5.	5.	5.	5.
Parents/carers need to:					
Student needs to:					

Example A				
Objectives	Unable to meet task requirements	Able to meet task requirements with assistance	Able to meet task requirements independently to age norm	Comments
Catch a football from 2 metres with two hands				
Stand on one leg for 20 seconds without wavering				
Sit quietly between activities				

Example B
Name: Class:
Crab Races:
Monday:
Tuesday:
Wednesday:
Thursday:
Friday:
Action:

Example C			
Objective	Strengths	Needs	Action
Crab walk: Monday: Tuesday: Wednesday: Thursday: Friday:			

Example D			
Objective			
CAN DO		CAN NOT DO	
Well	Just	Almost	Not close
1	2	3	4

Example E
Name
Group Leaders
Dates of Group
Aims:
Indicators: 0 = Unable to achieve 1 = Able to achieve with maximum assistance 2 = Able to achieve with moderate assistance 3 = Able to achieve with minimal assistance 4 = Independent 5 = Consistent

Performance Record Date:								
Objectives:								
Crab walk	0	1	1	2	2	3	4	5
Walk along bench	1	1	1	2	2	3	4	5
Stand on one leg	0	0	0	1	1	1	1	2

Functional, Component and Quiz Indicator Rating
Aim: To improve concentration 0 = Does not concentrate throughout session 1 = Minimal concentration span within session 2 = Concentrates for short length of time 3 = Concentrates for up to half of session 4 = Concentrates for most of session 5 = Concentrates for all of session

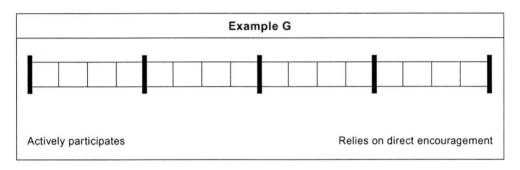

Example F

Attention

1	2	3	4	5	6	7	8	9	10
❑	❑	❑	❑	❑	❑	❑	❑	❑	❑

Is easily distracted   Is able to ignore distraction

Completes any activity

Example G

Actively participates   Relies on direct encouragement

Discussion – What methods of recording effectiveness and outcome of intervention exist in your work environment?

References

Arnheim, D.D. and Sinclair, W. A. (1979) *The Clumsy Child: A programme of motor therapy*. St Louis, MO: Mosby.

Bayley, N. (1969) Bayley Scales of Infant Development. New York: Psychological Corporation.

Bellman, M. *et al*. (1996) Schedule of Growing Skills II. Windsor: NFER-Nelson.

Bouffard, M. and Wall, A.E. (1990) 'A problem solving approach to movement skill acquisition: implications for special populations', in G. Reid (ed.) *Problems in movement control*, pp. 107–31. New York: North-Holland.

Bouffard, M., Watkinson, E.J., Thompson, L.P., Causgrove-Dunn, J.L. and Romanow, S.K.E. (1996) 'A test of the activity deficit hypothesis with children with movement difficulties', *Adapted Physical Activity Quarterly*, **13**, 61–73.

Bruininks, R. (1978) *Bruininks-Oseretsky Test of Motor Proficiency, Examiner's Manua*l. Circle Pines, MN: American Guidance Service.

Burton, A.W. and Davis, W.E. (1996) 'Ecological task analysis: utilising intrinsic measures in research and practice', *Human Movement Science*, **15**, 285–314.

Cantell, M.H., Smyth, M.M. and Ahonen, T.P. (1994) 'Clumsiness in adolescence: educational, motor, and social outcomes of motor delay detected at 5 years', *Adapted Physical Activity Quarterly*, **11**, 115–29.

Case-Smith, J. (2001) 'Use of standardised tests in paediatric practice', in J. Case-Smith (ed.) *Occupational Therapy for Children*, pp. 217–45. Missouri: Mosby.

Causgrove Dunn, J. and Watkinson, E.J. (1994) 'A study of the relationship between physical awkwardness and children's perceptions of physical competence', *Adapted Physical Activity Quarterly*, **11**, 275–83.

Cermak, A. and Larkin, D. (2000) *Developmental Co-ordination Disorder*. Canada: Delmar.

Coster, W., Deeney, T., Haltiwanger, J. and Haley, S. (1998) *School Function Assessment*. San Antonio, TX: Psychological Corporation.

Crawford, S.G., Wilson, B.N. and Dewey, D. (2001) *Identifying Developmental Co-ordination Disorder: Consistency between tests. Children with Developmental Co-ordination Disorder: Strategies for Success*. Canada: Hawthorn Press.

Davis, W.E. and Burton, A.W. (1991) 'Ecological task analysis: translating movmement behaviour theory into practice', *Adapted Physical Activity Quarterly*, **8**, 154–77.

Davis, W.E. and van Emmerik, R.E.A. (1995) 'An ecological task analysis approach for understanding motor development in mental retardation: research questions and strategies', in A. Vermeer and W.E. Davies (eds) *Physical and Motor Development in Mental Retardation*, pp. 33–66. Basel, Switzerland: Karger.

De Clive-Lowe, S. (1996) 'Outcome measurement, cost effectiveness and clinical audit – the importance of standardised assessment to occupational therapists in meeting new demands', *British Journal of Therapy*, **59** (8), 357–62.

Dwyer, C. and McKenzie, B.E. (1994) 'Impairment of visual memory in children who are clumsy', *Adapted Physical Activity Quarterly*, **11**, 179–89.

Faraone, S.F., Biederman, J. and Milberger, S. (1995) 'How reliable are maternal reports of their children's psychopathology? One year recall of psychiatric diagnoses of ADHD children', *Journal of American Academy of Adolescence and Psychiatry*, **34**, 1001.

Fisher, A.G. (1999) *The Assessment of Motor Process Skills*. Colorado: Three Star Press.

Frankenburg, W.K., Dodds, J.B. (1967) 'The Denver Developmental Screening Test', *Journal of Paediatrics*, **71**, 181–91.

Frankenburg, W.K. *et al.* (1990) *Denver II Technical Manual*. Denver, CO: Denver Developmental Materials Inc.

Gallahue, D.L. and Ozmun, J.C. (1995) *Understanding Motor Development*, 3rd edn. Madison, WI: Brown & Benchmark.

Gentile, A.M. (1992) 'The nature of skill acquisition: therapeutic implications for children with movement disorders', *Medical Sports Science*, **36**, 31–40.

Geuze, R.H. and Borger, H. (1993) 'Children who are clumsy: five years later', *Adapted Physical Activity Quarterly*, **10**, 10–21.

Geuze, R.H. and Kalverboer, A.F. (1987) 'Inconsistency and adaptation in timing of clumsy children', *Journal of Human Movement Studies*, **13**, 421–32.

Glascoe, F.P. and Dworkin, P.H. (1995) 'The role of parents in the detection of developmental and behavioural problems', *Pediatrics*, **95**, 829–36.

Gredler, G. (1992) *School Readiness: Assessment and educational issues*. Brandom, VT: Clinical Psychology Publishing.

Gredler, G. (1997) 'Issues in early childhood screening and assessment', *Psychology in Schools*, **34** (2), 99–105.

Gubbay, S. (1975) *The Clumsy Child: A study of developmental apraxia and agnosic ataxia*, p. 17. London: Saunders.

Haley, S., Coster, W., Ludlow, L., Haltiwanger, J. and Andrellos, P. (1992) *Pediatric Evaluation of Disability Inventory (PEDI): Development, Standardisation and Administration Manual*. SF.

Haubenstricker, J. *et al.* (1981) 'The efficiency of the Bruininks-Oseretsky Test of Motor Proficiency in discriminating between normal children and those with gross motor dysfunction'. Paper presented at the Motor Development Academy at the AAHPERD Convention, Boston, MA.

Henderson, S. and Sugden, D. (1992) *Movement ABC Battery for Children Manual*. London: Psychological Corporation.

Kadesjo, B. and Gillberg, C. (1999) 'Developmental coordination disorder in Swedish 7-year-old children', *Journal of American Child Adolescence and Psychiatry*, **38** (7), 820–8.

Keogh, J.F., Sugden, D., Reynard, C.L. and Calkins, J. (1979) 'Identifcation of clumsy children: comparisons and comments', *Journal of Human Movment Studies*, **5**, 32–41.

Laszlo, J.I., Bairstow, P. and Bartrip, J. (1988) 'A new approach to treatment of perceptuo-motor dysfunction: previously called "clumsiness"', *Support for Learning*, **3**, 35–40.

Law, M. and Letts, L. (1989) 'A critical review of scales of activities of daily living', *The American Journal of Occupational Therapy*, **43**, 522–8.

Losse, A., Henderson, S.E., Elliman, D., Hall, D., Knight, E. and Jongmans, M. (1991) 'Clumsiness in children – do they grow out of it? A 10-year follow-up study', *Developmental Medicine and Child Neurology*, **33**, 55–68.

Maeland, A.F. (1992) 'Handwriting and perceptual-motor skills in clumsy, dysgraphic, and normal children'. *Perceptual and Motor Skills*, **75**, 1207–17.

Mandich, A.D., Polatajko, H., Macnab, J. and Miller, L.T. (2001) *Treatment of Children with Developmental Co-ordination Disorder: what is the evidence?* Canada: Hawthorn Press.

McClenaghan, B.A. (1976) 'Development of an observational instrument to assess selected fundamental movement patterns of low motor functioning children'. Unpublished Doctoral Dissertation, Indiana University.

McClenaghan, B.A. and Gallahue, D.L. (1978) *Observation and assessment.* Philadelphia: W.B. Saunders.

Miller, L.T., Missiuna, C.A., Macnab, J.J., Malloy-Miller, T. and Polatajko, H.J. (2001) 'Clinical description of children with Developmental Coordination Disorder', *Canadian Journal of Occupational Therapy Abstracts,* **68** (1).

Missiuna, C. and Pollock, N. (1995) 'Beyond the norms: need for multiple sources of data in the assessment of children', *Physical and Occupational Therapy in Pediatrics,* **15** (4), 57–71.

Murphy, J.B. and Gliner, J.A. (1988) 'Visual and motor sequencing in normal and clumsy children', *Occupational Therapy Journal of Research,* **8**, 89–103.

Ovretveit, J. (1998) *Evaluating Health Intervention.* Buckingham: Open University Press.

Pollock, N. and Stewart, D. (1998) 'Occupational performance needs of school-aged children with physical disabilities in the community', *Physical & Occupational Therapy in Pediatrics,* **18**, 55–68.

Revie and Larkin (1993) 'Task specific intervention with children reduces movement problems', *Adapted Physical Activity Quarterly,* **10**, 29–4.

Roach, E.G. and Kephart, Newall C. (1966) *The Purdue Perceptual Motor Survey (PPMS).* USA: Charles E. Merrill Publishing Co.

Schoemaker, M.M. and Kalverboer, A.F. (1994) 'Social and affective problems of children who are clumsy: how early do they begin?', *Adapted Physical Activity Quarterly,* **11**, 130–40.

Seefeldt, V. and Haubenstricker, J. (1976) 'Developmental sequences of fundamental motor skills', Unpublished research, Michigan State University.

Seefeldt, V. and Haubenstricker, J. (1982) *The Development of Movement Control and Co-ordination.* New York: John Wiley & Sons.

Smyth, M.M. and Mason, U.C. (1998) 'The use of proprioception in normal and clumsy children', *Developmental Medicine and Child Neurology,* **40**, 672–81.

Sudgen, D.A. and Keogh, J.F. (1990) *Problems in Movement Skill Development.* Columbia, SC: USC Press.

Ulrich, B. (1985) *Test of Gross Motor Development.* Austin TX: Pro Ed.

Van der Meulen, J.H.P., Denier van der Gon, J.J., Gielen, C.C.A.M., Gooskens, R.H.J.M. and Willemse, J. (1991) 'Visuomotor performance of normal and clumsy children. II: Arm tracking with and without visual feedback', *Developmental Medicine and Child Neurology,* **33**, 118–29.

Volman, M.J. and Geuze, R.H. (1998) 'Stability of rhythmic finger movement in children with a developmental coordination disorder', *Motor Control,* **2** (1), 34–60.

Zittle, L. (1994) 'Gross motor assessment of pre-school children with special needs: instrumental considerations', *Adapted Physical Activity Quarterly,* **11**, 245–60.

CHAPTER 5

The primary school child

Learning objectives
- To gain an understanding of the implications for a child with DCD in the classroom and at home.
- To gain an understanding of how the child can access the curriculum.
- To consider the impact school has on home behaviour and vice versa.

Learning outcomes
- To consider how to manage the child at home and in the classroom effectively, working as part of a team.
- To reflect on the child's difficulties and consider what changes need to be made in the living and learning environment.

Introduction

Inclusion is not episodic – inclusion is 'belonging'. (McCormick & Schiefelbusch 1997)

The child has a right to be helped to fulfil his potential in a setting which sees both him and his peers in a positive light. (Drifte 2001)

At preschool level a DCD child may present with high activity levels, and awkward movement skills both at a gross and fine level. Their play skills may still lack imagination and creativity. The language may be at a level which appears to be fine, as the child is only using high frequency words. However, when he or she now has to tackle and consider more complex conversations and a greater number of interactions, they may show increased difficulties.

At this stage it may not be easy to identify any major difficulties with the child's performance skills and their ability may be seen as reasonably consistent with their peers. Any gap may not be that great, and expectations not so high. In addition, if the child is a boy, it is possible that his acquisition and mastery of everyday living and learning skills is due to his sex, i.e. boys develop at a slower rate than girls. At this stage any delay is commonly responded to as 'well he's a boy, and he'll soon grow out of it'.

At primary school, the environment now becomes more structured. Activities which could have been avoided in a playgroup or nursery setting, now have to be confronted head on as they are integral to the curriculum. Here the child has to handle and deal with increasing amounts of information and demands upon their sensory motor skills. However if the child has not established good foundation skills, i.e. the individual building blocks and scaffolding, their performance and productivity will be compromised. This is like being asked to build a tower that has no foundations – it starts to wobble and possibly falls!

The DCD child is likely to have deficits in their ability to play. Certainly, work by Primeau (1992) and Bouffard *et al.* (1996) has shown that children with DCD are likely to participate less than their peers, are less vigorously active, and may play less on large equipment. These early experiences are likely to have a lasting effect in school in terms of peer interaction and self-worth. There is a body of research which suggests that the DCD child tends to be more passive in play and more anxious than other children. Bundy (2002), however, suggests that the child is seen joining in games and activities with other children, but may not be gaining the same enjoyment. She further suggests that as the child is likely to be less competent, then they are less accepted by their peers. This leads to isolation and reinforces feelings of low self-worth.

Most children commence school with a variety of experiences, both socially and culturally. If they do not have difficulty acquiring and mastering skills it is suggested that they are able to catch up with their peers in the first few terms. However, the child with DCD may still be struggling even after being at school for a year. Nevertheless, even at this stage it may not be reasonable to 'pin' a label on the child, as professionals and carers need to be mindful of different 'conditions' that may present with similar features at this stage.

In view of the range of normal development, it is usually when a child enters formal education that the differences between the child with DCD and his or her peers become more evident. It is at this point that concerns are generally raised and the intervention process begins.

School

Transitions

When considering 'transition' within this context, it is all too common to think of that period from junior to secondary school, or from school to work. However, it is important to bear in mind that transitional periods occur all through life. For all individuals this can be daunting, let alone those with more special needs.

Even at a young age, separating from parents may be stressful for the child who does not have the basic skills in place, e.g. independently going to the toilet, changing clothes for PE, playing with other children, basic ball skills. The world can feel like a very frightening place, and it may be all too easy to think lightly of the tantrums and crying, let alone if the behaviour becomes protracted, and subsequently 'irritating'.

Starting school

Some children with DCD will enter school full of enthusiasm and eager to explore; others will be more reticent and nervous. Many children will be able to cope with a full day/session, but others will not. This may be due to difficulty separating from the mother, lack of experience, e.g. has limited early experience of interacting with other children such as going to playgroup or mothers and toddlers. Some children may already be showing signs of being aware that they are in some way different from their peers. This transition period requires forward planning in order to allow the child to be prepared with adequate skills and to be able to gain opportunities to positively experience each area of the curriculum, and for the teacher to gain an understanding of the level of the child's strengths and weaknesses.

Many parents of children with DCD and other coexisting difficulties can often be viewed as over-anxious parents. In the early years the difficulties for the child may not yet have come to light, or, if they have, the parent may not have come to terms with the diagnosis. This may be a difficult time of adjustment. The parents may see their child as not being what they had expected. Future plans may now seem to be dashed and there may be a period of grieving. This may present in school as a parent with frustration, guilt and resentment towards the child and who also wants to over-protect their child (Bundy 2002).

Professionals involved in early years services, including play leaders, child-minders, health visitors, nursery nurses, all play a key role in not only identifying potential difficulties for the child with special needs but also in supporting the parents through a difficult and turbulent period. The following can assist greatly in providing parents with support:

- give them time to talk;

- be prepared to listen;
- provide information that they can take away and an opportunity to come back and ask further questions;
- be honest about what you are seeing with the child but not giving predictions for the future, as each child can be very different despite having a label;
- explain what is happening – keep them up to date;
- work together – gain collaboration from others working with the child and link services together for the parent;
- understand and keep up to date about DCD and other similar difficulties;
- put together a resource box, so that parents can have some ideas of activities they can do at home;
- keep a record of local resources and agencies.

Parents are the child's first and most enduring educators (QCA 2000). The learning process does not exclusively take place at school, home or in the clinical setting. Therefore the role of the professional and the parent are inextricably linked and, as such, supporting the parent is likely to increase any successful intervention in school.

> **Discussion** – What other methods can be used to ensure effective communication between home and school?

Key difficulties affecting the child's performance

There are many key difficulties at this stage that can affect the child's performance. In school difficulties can arise from the following factors:

- Classrooms are often very busy and noisy places.
- Chairs and tables are usually grouped together and children work alongside each other in learning sets.
- In some classes children may not always be facing towards the teacher. This is often true in the primary school where children may be seated at hexagonal tables with their back to the teacher some of the time.
- Having to look up and turn around to see the teacher may result in the child losing their place and losing ability to concentrate.
- The child may only hear the ends of instructions and seem confused about tasks they are expected to do. They may be having difficulty sequencing auditory input, which leaves them with gaps in information, e.g. hearing the first and last part of an instruction but not the middle part, as each component takes longer to process.

- The child with DCD may find negotiating their way around tables and chairs difficult to do, and knock into people and objects.
- Workbooks and tools may be stored in a personal tray away from the child's 'seat', requiring him or her to get up and down to complete tasks. This may make the child more disorganised.
- The child with DCD may have problems with 'looking', 'listening' and 'doing' at the same time.
- They may find it harder to integrate these components for many curricular activities such as copying from the board, and following a series of instructions which require an action.
- To the observer, the child with DCD may not appear to be giving their best effort, although for the child in many cases what they are doing *is* their best effort. They may therefore be penalised for this by being remonstrated for untidy work, resulting in being kept in at breaktime to finish it or being given extra homework to take home at the end of the day. This may be an added burden, which tips the child over and can result in him or her not being able to cope. This then has a knock-on effect by producing negative behaviour at home.

Difficulty can stem from *posture*:

- Sitting still at the table – the child may be seen sitting at the table in a number of positions. Some children may be seen holding on to the table to increase stability, slumped at the table, or stretched out with arms extended to gain stability.

Difficulties connected with *behaviour* include:

- The child may use 'opt out' or 'cover up' strategies such as clowning around or not bothering with some tasks where they know that they may fail or have failed in the past.
- Not understanding what is required and seeming to 'switch off', appearing vacant. This may be occasionally thought of as a sign of epilepsy (petit mal). If symptoms persist, then this should be considered.
- Difficulty staying on task – however there is a need to make sure that the child's underlying difficulties are understood. Does the child have postural difficulties and need to concentrate on balancing on the chair; a language difficulty not understanding commands; or a perceptual difficulty in not being able to interpret the sensory information around him or her?
- Organising his or her thoughts while doing written work.

- Unable to complete work – this may be interpreted as being lazy but this may reflect that the child is having difficulty integrating their thoughts under time pressures. Is this seen in all environments and classes or just in one area? How does that inform you of the child's difficulties?
- Not being able to work cooperatively in a group setting. The child may want to lead the activity so that they remain in control. However, they may not have the organisational skills or the ability to record information at speed to do this successfully, as well as being a poor negotiator. The child may be seen to be sidelined by their peers and end up being more isolated.

Difficulties relating to *writing* are:

- Presentation may be poor and illegible to others and even to the child them-selves. Their best writing may never be good enough to use, especially once they are at secondary school and required to record information at speed.
- Organisation of work on paper.
- Poor letter formation, letter reversals – the writing may vary in size and quality from the top of the page to the bottom. The letters may go above and below lines on the page. The constancy of shape and form may be difficult to maintain. The child's ability to write neatly may vary at different times of the day. Usually the child is better in the morning when less tired.

Difficulties in *mathematics* might be:

- The child may show problems with sequencing and remembering times tables. He or she may need to see how things work in order to gain an under-standing of abstract and 3D concepts.

Difficulties of a *social* nature can include:

- The child may not seem to be good at winning or losing a game, and may leave a situation inappropriately without warning.
- The child may be unaware of his or her appearance, e.g. the fact their shirt is hanging out or their nose is running.
- The child may appear sloppy with his or her feet shuffling along, or be seen to slouch in a seat. This may be due to lower muscle tone, and makes it harder for the child to keep upright and maintain a good posture.

Where a child has difficulty accessing a learning or a living skill it is important to consider not just what 'the problem is', but also to consider what the underlying factors are that may be influencing the child's responses. For example, consider handwriting difficulties. When examining this aspect an assumption is generally made about the quality of a child's work, i.e. neatness (which may relate to pencil control), content, or spelling. Remediation may then take the form of handwriting practice or spelling activities. However, Figure 5.1 considers the foundation skills for handwriting where it is possible that any one of the building blocks may not be firmly established. Therefore it may not be the pencil control that needs remediating while sat at the table in class; but more gross motor control, which needs to be remediated through PE or small group work.

Observing the way in which a child approaches a task will often give an indication of the way in which a child prefers to learn. It is important to remember that all individuals learn in different ways and that when 'teaching' a child activities should be presented in a multisensory format. It is also possible that the teacher's 'teaching' style is different from the child's 'learning' style. A flexible approach is therefore needed.

It is also important to remember that remedying a problem is likely to take some

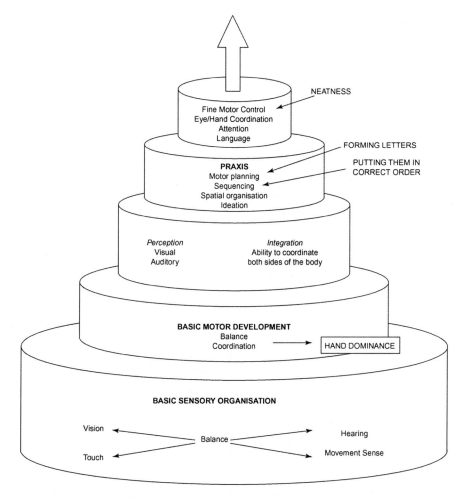

Figure 5.1   Building blocks for handwriting

time. In most cases, where appropriate, it is necessary to find short-term *practical* solutions to ensure that the child is able to maintain pace with his or her peers but also, and importantly, maintain confidence and self-esteem. Not all solutions suit all children and the skill of the teacher is to be innovative in approach. Many techniques or tools used for other children with 'conditions' may be suitable for the DCD child.

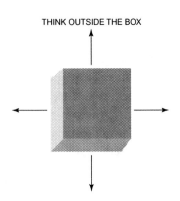

THINK OUTSIDE THE BOX

Types of learners

- Visual/verbal – These learners like to read the written word. They like books, posters, slogans, instructional material with clearly written text.
- Auditory – These learners like to hear information through spoken explanations, commentaries, tapes. They benefit from reading aloud and making tapes.
- Physical – These learners like hands-on learning where they can immediately try things for themselves. They like to do as they learn. This includes doodling and fiddling.

Children with DCD often have coexisting features of other difficulties such as language problems and visual perceptual problems, as well as their movement problems. In many cases, these children's learning abilities can be significantly compromised in a classroom situation. It is no wonder that they 'switch off' or become the class clown.

> **Discussion** – In the classroom setting, what practical strategies and approaches could be used to enable the child with DCD?

Impact of the problem	Solution	Resources/approaches required
Cutting with scissors	Choice of suitable tools Graded scissor programme	PETA Scissor Craft Contact local Occupational Therapist

PE and games

The child with DCD will classically find that PE and other games in school one of the most stressful areas of their day. Getting changed, negotiating instructions, running in different directions and working as a part of a team will all stretch the competency of a child that may already be overstretched.

It is likely that the child will not have the foundation skills in place to take part in all activities with the same skill and control as their peers. These activities serve to further accentuate his or her differences. More than likely at this age the child is aware that he or she is 'not as good as the other children'. It is probable that they will not be picked for the team and any feelings of inadequacy will be confirmed by hearing the whispers from others. Exposure at sports day in front of greater numbers of children and adults may be the final straw. The three-legged race for a child who cannot balance on two legs, or the dressing-up race, may not be best for the child with DCD!

In PE and games the child could well experience problems relating to the following:

- His or her motor foundation skills are usually weaker and generally they may not have the ability to make subtle postural adjustments for balance and coordination.
- Understanding the lesson plan, as he or she may have missed vital instructions about what is required.
- Motivating themselves as he or she may find others laugh at them when they try to do a task in front of other children.
- Stopping in a controlled way when running.
- Understanding the language required for movement and position, such as on, in, through, backward, under.
- Navigating their body accurately around the gym or when using PE equipment. They may have a poor sense of body awareness resulting in bumping into things as well as other children.
- Listening and moving at the same time – they may end up watching others and trying to copy them rather than understanding what to do themselves.
- Climbing and using equipment that is off the floor – walking along a beam, for example, may make the child anxious.
- Grading movements in a smooth manner.
- Hopping, skipping and jumping – taking their weight on one leg and remaining stable.
- Getting changed at the end of the class, when this may make them late for their next class.

Discussion – How could the child with DCD be enabled to fully participate in a PE session?

Problem	Impact	Solution	Resources required
Cannot stand on one leg	Cannot hop/kick a ball	Practise stepping up and over Kick a big ball from a standing position	Use low level PE equipment Ask advice from OT/Physiotherapist

Inclusion and the DCD child

The legislative process within the educational setting has pledged its commitment to the diversity of these and other pupils with special educational needs in its document *Excellence for all Children* (DfEE 1997), which states that 'all children in a mainstream class must be capable of joining fully with their peers in the curriculum and social life of the school', while 'separate provision may be necessary on occasion for specific purposes and inclusion must encompass teaching and curriculum appropriate to the child's needs'.

The Green Paper *The Best for Special Education* (1997), emphasises the importance of meeting the needs of all children with special educational needs, with the focus on raising levels of attainment for such children. Local Education Authorities now have to include details of action to support children with SEN together with arrangements for monitoring standards among such children. The *inclusive approach* is based on the understanding that everyone belongs and that it is inappropriate to design standard programmes and expect them to 'fit' every child. Instead the emphasis is placed on 'fitting the programme' to what the child needs. No one is excluded, and every child is valued as an individual. Furthermore, the approach is to find ways for every child to participate and be successful. For this approach to be fully embraced, the following underpinning factors should apply:

- for teachers to learn about special needs and how to meet these needs within the context of the daily routine;
- the child is able to be maintained within the physical dimensions of the classroom and curriculum delivery;
- that, as much as possible, the activities should be the same as those in which the other children are participating;
- that the social aspects of the curriculum and school are also encompassed.

Discussion – Do children with DCD require additional physical support in order that they can fully access the curriculum, and if so what should this be and how should it be delivered? What are the barriers to inclusion?

Home

It is likely that the child with DCD has had to concentrate and work much more than twice as hard as the other children in his or her class. As they leave the school they may feel a sense of relief. This may be expressed as a tantrum before he or she has even left the school gates. The child has often been well behaved in school but then expresses their frustrations when they get home, in what they see as a safe environment. The already tired child may be bringing home extra work that he or she has not been able to complete during the school day, and may feel over-whelmed. He or she may be well behaved in school but badly behaved at home.

The child may have difficulties with:

- Remembering their homework and the correct tools to do the job.
- Organising their work – the task may just seem too great to even know where to start.
- Recording their homework.
- Attending to the work – they may have poor concentration and appear fidgety.
- Talking about their feelings – these may be 'acted out', for example shouting at Mum or starting a fight with a sister or brother.

The child is likely to have difficulties with everyday living skills such as:

- Self-organisation.
- Dressing – buttons and small fastenings may be difficult to do. Placing clothes in the right order may also be a challenge. This may end up in the parent 'doing for the child', causing increased anxiety in the household and a child arriving in school already stressed by the early morning's activities.
- Sleep – the child may be sleep-disordered. This may have an impact on their ability to function in school.
- Personal care – using the toilet, cleaning teeth, brushing hair, washing face and hands.
- Eating and drinking – using cutlery, drinking from a cup.
- Independence skills – buttering toast, pouring a drink, making a simple cold drink.

Discussion – What strategies can be provided to enable the child at home?

Problem	Solution	Resource required
Difficulty managing cutlery	Use smaller and fatter-handled cutlery	Caring cutlery (Boots the Chemist) Children's cutlery (Ikea)
Poor awareness of time	Use timers or buzzer alarms	Kitchen timers Stopwatches

Working together

Partnerships with families

> A happy and open relationship with parents, based on confidence and trust, is crucial to the building of a successful relationship with their children. (Whitbread 1996)

The new Code of Practice on Special Educational Needs places emphasis on initiatives promoting parents as partners in the process. This is further supported by the document *Shaping the Future for Special Education* (Welsh Office 1999), which states 'the most effective results are achieved where parents, school and LEAs work in partnership, within a clear framework'. More recently, research conducted by Professor David Sugden (Sugden and Chambers 2001) highlights that training parents and teachers can be just as effective as having a session with an occupational therapist or physiotherapist. Further, Nickse (1990) stated that the impact of educational programming is likely to be more profound and lasting if the whole family is involved.

Home Liaison Parent Partnerships
This helps to:

- establish positive links between home and the school setting;
- develop the relationship between child and staff;
- familiarise parents with the aims of the setting;
- enables the professional to become aware of home circumstances and relevant prior experience;
- informally assess a child's skills.

Parents may feel they are being blamed for their child's difficulties when issues are first raised and questions asked of them. Parental involvement should include options that reflect each family's own culture, strengths, values, skills and expectations. Readers are referred to Chapter 4 regarding parental involvement in the assessment/intervention process.

Partnerships with professionals
Services for children with DCD need to be organised in a coherent and coordinated manner if they are to be effective. This can often be quite difficult as it is possible that one family may have many agencies involved. The Department for Education (DfEE 1997) recognised this need and called for close cooperation between schools, LEAs, the health services and social services. The Education Act 1993 also called for interagency cooperation.

An absence or lack of integration and coordination of services for children with

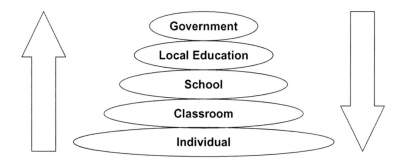

Figure 5.2   A top down/bottom up approach to collaborative working

DCD can be very frustrating for parents. It can also lead to fragmented and even conflicting information about their child. In addition to coordination across agencies, coordination must also occur across levels of government, with consistency assured between policies developed at state and at local levels.

A truly collaborative relationship goes beyond cooperation and coordination and involves a greater commitment of time and resources (Bruder 1994).

Barriers to collaboration
The following can be serious barriers to collaboration:

- Staff, time, budget limitations
- Poor communication skills
- Competitiveness
- Lack of incentive
- Lack of training
- Preoccupation with administration
- Resistance to change
- Lack of political awareness
- Territorial issues
- Lack of information or awareness about local services or other professionals' roles
- Poor team dynamics
- Poor planning and organisation
- Poor audit and monitoring of processes
- Logistical issues
- Lack of administrative support
- Jargon – no common language

Discussion – What steps can be taken to minimise the barriers between interagency and parental partnerships?

References

Bouffard, M., Watkinson, E.J., Thompson, L.P., Causgrove Dunn, J.L. and Romanolo S.K.E. (1996) 'A test of the activity deficit hypothesis with children with movement difficulties', *Adapted Physical Activity Quarterly*, **13**, 61–73.

Bruder, M.B. (1994) 'Working with members of other disciplines – collaboration for success' in M. Wolery and J.S. Wilbers (eds) *Including Children with Special Needs in Early Childhood Programme*, pp. 45–70. Washington, DC: National Association for the Education of Young Children.

Bundy, A . (2002) 'Play and children with DCD: what we know, what we suspect', 5th Biennial Conference Developmental Co-ordination Disorders, Banff, Alberta, Canada.

Department for Education (1997) *Excellence for All Children*, Consultative Green Paper. HMSO.

Drifte, C. (2001) *Special Needs in Early Years Settings – a Guide for Practitioners*. London: David Fulton Publishers.

McCormick, L., Schiefelbusch, R.L. (1997) *Supporting Children with Communication Difficulties in Inclusive Settings*. Boston, MA: Allyn and Bacon.

Nickse, R.S. (1990) 'Family and intergenerational literacy programs', Information Series No. 342, ERIC Clearing House on Adult Careers and Vocational Education (ED 327736), Columbus.

Primeau, L. (1992) 'Game playing behaviour in children with developmental dyspraxia', Unpublished Masters Dissertation, University of Southern California.

QCA (2000) *Curriculum Guidance for the Foundation Stage*. London: Qualifications Curriculum Authority.

Sugden, D. and Chambers, M. (2001) 'Stability and change following intervention in children with DCD', Keynote Lecture, DCD-V Conference Mechanisms, Measurement and Management, Banff, Alberta.

Whitbread, D. (1996) *Teaching and Learning in the Early Years*. London: Routledge.

CHAPTER 6

The adolescent – a time of transition

Learning objectives
- To understand the key elements in the management of transition from primary to secondary school.
- To consider the impact that puberty has on the child with DCD.
- To critically evaluate the requirements for aids and adaptations in the classroom and the home setting to assist management.
- To develop and deliver an Individual Educational Plan within an appropriate educational environment.
- To critically evaluate the social and psychological impact on an individual with DCD in the context of the type of management given.

Learning outcomes
- To be able to construct an appropriate management plan so that home, school and the pupil are considered.
- To advise about aids and adaptations for the child in secondary school.

Discussion – Before reading the whole chapter: Consider a school day from the time the adolescent gets up, until bedtime – what difficulties do you think the individual with DCD will meet during each day?

Getting up in the morning	
Breakfast	
Packing bags and books	
Sandwiches	
Arrival at school	
Different classes, e.g. mathematics, cookery, chemistry	
Breaktime	
Lunchtime	
Sport	
Recording	
Travel home	
Homework	
Bedtime	

The adolescent

Teenage years are a time of trial and tribulation as the teenager is learning to adapt to changes both emotionally and physically. For individuals with specific learning difficulties the time is made worse by trying to cope with many of the problems that they may have encountered in primary school, but are now accentuated as they move into the secondary school system. They may be less emotionally mature than their peers.

The young adolescent wants to be like their peers but may not be able to refine their skills and work in a social situation with confidence. They may be happiest at home. This is quite different from the behaviour that most teenagers would display. Often they would want to actively try to increase their distance from their parents and even try to disown them if they could!

Poorer social skills partnered with coordination difficulties mean the gap widens far more than at primary school and self-esteem and confidence are badly bruised at a vulnerable stage in development.

Transition

Transition causes different sets of difficulties at each stage moving from adolescence to adulthood. Key times are:

- From primary to secondary school
- From secondary school to further/higher education
- Leaving home and gaining independent living skills
- Gaining employment and staying in employment
- Forming relationships.

Transition difficulties – from primary to secondary school

The attitudes of teachers and peers to the child with DCD when he or she arrives at a new school are likely to prove significant. He or she might be regarded as being:

- a difficult child (pre-labelled) rather than a child with difficulties;
- a child with DCD – but teachers may have a lack of understanding of the label and its implications for the child and how this will affect him or her in different, new lessons such as Chemistry or Cookery;
- a low achiever, rather than having specific difficulties.

The move to secondary school means a number of major changes for all children. Most children will cope with these and feel accustomed to the changes by the end of the first couple of weeks. In contrast, the child with DCD may take two to three terms to learn to navigate their way around the school and may require ongoing support throughout their school days to allow them to fully access the curriculum.

If there has been little preparation for the huge changes that occur between primary and secondary school this leaves the child floundering and results in difficulties for the child in accessing the curriculum and makes it much harder for him or her to make friends. The first few weeks are crucial in developing the new peer group and poor preparation can result in lasting damage throughout the secondary school days.

Initial enthusiasm to support the child may disappear when there is an underlying feeling that the child should be able to go it alone. 'How many times should he be shown?', 'Can't he understand it by now', 'I am not going to mother him any longer' are phrases that have been uttered from time to time. However, an analogy could be to consider how one would support a person with visual impairment who uses a white stick – we would not consider taking the stick away from them after a few weeks because they had mastered their way around and should not need it any longer! In some ways DCD is similar – it does not just go away. However the DCD child does not walk around with a marker of his or her difficulties so is often seen as lazy, stupid or not really trying as hard as he or she could. The aspect of continuing support is one that is crucial for some children and is again essential into adulthood, where low level but continuing intervention can make the difference between success and failure, and where there are constant choices and changes occurring, impacting on the decision-making process. There is evidence to show that DCD persists at least into adolescence (e.g. Cantell *et al.* 1994, Losse *et al.* 1991, Gillberg *et al.* 1989).

The process of change

Change in the school environment can make the individual have major 'wobbles' and make him or her anxious. Anxiety about lack of control of their environment can lead to the individual feeling panicky all of the time and have a knock-on effect on their performance. They may lash out at others or withdraw into themselves in a form of self-protection.

Secondary schools are often places of change. Desks and chairs are moved in the class, new teachers coming in to cover lessons. This causes additional strains on the child who is also trying to cope with their underlying difficulties and now has more problems layered on top. This can result in a breakdown in the child's mechanisms for coping and is why we sometimes see secondary school being a crisis time, after the child has seemingly being able to cope in primary school.

The move to secondary school exposes the child at key times in the school day, such as coping alone in the playground at break and lunchtimes. He or she can no longer cover up their difficulties by looking as if helping the younger children. Teachers may not be present all of the time to supervise in the same way as in the primary school playground and not all teachers in a large school will be aware of the child's difficulties.

Key transition difficulties
Key difficulties include:

- Negotiating the way around school – the child may get lost and this may result in being late for class.
- Meeting new children who may not understand their difficulties.
- Meeting new teachers who do not recognise they have difficulties.
- Learning about the rules of the school – explicit and implicit.
- Learning new teachers' names and their expectations and styles of teaching.
- Learning about the timetable and the appropriate books and tools required.
- Carrying equipment around all day – no central place to return to, therefore increasing the chances of losing equipment or having incorrect equipment for the next class.
- Coping with change determined by others not themselves.
- Independently organising their work and managing their own timetable.
- Being competent at ball skills/dressing and undressing as they are expected to cope with more complex tasks.
- Being less supervised in the playground and at lunchtime – so the child is able to wander around on their own more (not seeking social interaction) or be more open to being bullied by others.
- Coping with new topics they have not studied before.

Discussion – Transition issues

- What type of baseline assessment is used to identify children that may have been missed in primary school?
- Critically evaluate in your school or in another local school how the IEP (Individual Education Plan) is constructed to ensure that targets are deliverable, and structured in a way that understands the underlying difficulties?
- How is the child reassessed for improvement?
- How do you currently gain information about children coming into your school?
- Is this extensive enough to know which children will require additional assistance?
- How many children in your school are labelled 'as having dyspraxia/DCD'?
- How accurate do you think this is?
- Consider what labels are used in your school and whether they are diagnostic or functional?

Transition 'to do' list from primary to secondary school

1. Information should be transferred over so that all teachers know a profile of strengths and difficulties – could this be kept in a diary?
2. Visits to school should try to take place over two terms.
3. Draw up a map of school/give opportunity to take photos to become familiar with school setting.
4. Parents to be given the opportunity to visit the school.
5. Timetable given as soon as possible.
6. Baseline assessment undertaken to check where learning level is and level of remediation required.
7. Consideration of adaptations required for classroom/sport and new subjects.
8. Consideration of help required for organising work.
9. Consideration of help required in note-taking.
10. Consideration of where locker placed in school, and method to transport books and equipment.
11. Mentor/tutor introduced before new term.
12. Buddy system in place for first two terms.
13. Use of angle boards/position in class/amount of room required taken into consideration.
14. Adaptation of tools if required, such as protractors, rulers, pens.
15. Extra time allowed for homework.
16. Work written down for individual on an ongoing basis if required.
17. 'Three way communication card' between school – different teachers, with home and with the individual.
18. Help offered for girls with periods/personal hygiene.

Underlying difficulties

What underlying difficulties does the teenager with DCD have? There are three key areas to consider: home; school; social and personal.

The adolescent at home

It is often the parents who bear the brunt of the stress that the adolescent is going through rather than the school. It is quite normal to become oppositional at this stage in most children's lives. The child with DCD is going through many of the changes that their peers are trying to come to terms with, but has additional difficulties to cope with. They may also have other co-morbid learning difficulties that will impact on their ability to go through adolescence and on to adulthood smoothly.

Most adolescents require support and guidance at this stage in their lives, but want to reject it at the same time. For most individuals with DCD the individual is in no doubt that they are different from their peers.

These normal developmental changes impact on the child with DCD: puberty and periods; personal hygiene; sex; body awareness; make-up; choosing clothes; not sharing similar hobbies; lack of independent living skills.

Puberty and periods

- Girls have to cope with knowing when their periods will begin and then learn to get in a routine to remember when to change pads or tampons. As timing is a problem for many individuals this can be the first problem. Some girls forget to regularly change their sanitary products and may also seem to have a lack of awareness about disposal of pads in school. The girl may seem to lack the discretion that others guard so fiercely.
- Not being aware of when periods start each month may mean that some girls have accidents when in school, highlighting their difficulties very obviously to others.
- The girl may seem to lack the emotional responsibility for her own body.

Personal hygiene

Lack of social awareness, for example an action that is harmless at home, will cause mirth from peers if repeated in school.

- The adolescent may end up avoiding going to the toilet altogether, and may drink less during the day to minimise visits to the toilet. This may lead to additional difficulties with constipation.
- Difficulty with bottom wiping – teenagers often go through a 'dirty' stage and are more sweaty and smelly but they usually do not to have a 'toilety' smell. If they do, this can additionally lead them to be isolated from their peers.

Sex

There may be some difficulties using contraception, such as the pill. Lack of time concepts may make it difficult to remember to take it regularly. In addition, use of condoms – fitting a condom may be more difficult if coordination is not so good.

Lack of awareness of own body as well as others

Some adults with DCD have been noted to be uncomfortable with light touch by others and may not even have explored their own bodies before embarking on a relationship. This reticence in being touched may make it harder for the individual to establish successful relationships until he or she can learn about touch for themselves. Lack of social distance concepts may also mean that the individual comes too close and invades body space of others and is 'all or nothing' in his or her advances. Others may misinterpret this.

Make-up

- Using mascara for a girl may be difficult, as well as knowing how much make-up to apply and being even-handed.

Choosing clothes

- Choosing appropriate clothes for the occasion, and knowing that looking different will cause further problems for the individual. An insight into his or her own appearance may be lacking and also the understanding that blending in with peers is very important at this stage in life. Support and guidance may be required at this stage to allow the individual to develop their own style.

Not sharing similar hobbies with peers

- Adolescents are likely not to be as sporty as their peers and so may miss out on potential occasions where they can socialise and bond. They do not have the sporting language to join in conversation either.

Lack of independent living skills

- the individual may find it harder to prepare a snack for themselves – tasks like buttering bread, slicing bread, using a tin-opener may all be difficult
- handling money, especially when under pressure, e.g in a bus queue
- following a recipe in the correct order
- organising themselves and their room to find what they need, e.g clothes that match, socks the right colour
- travelling on public transport with confidence; they may find it harder to recognise which bus stop to get on and off at, or to take directions from someone else
- they may find remembering their address and telephone number difficult at times of stress.

School

The following difficulties may manifest themselves before the time of starting secondary school:

Socially inappropriate behaviour

- The adolescent may seem too honest and say things that may be taken in the wrong way. They may see things in a literal way and be quite moralistic and tell others of their beliefs.
- The adolescent may have low self-esteem, as they see others being asked to parties and out shopping, etc., but they are excluded. Less practice at being sociable and fewer opportunities lead to a self-fulfilling prophecy of being less socially able.

Emotional behaviour

Some or all of these behaviours may be displayed:

- Grabbing someone and not realising how hard or soft to do this.
- Hugging people who they may not know well, and not discriminating sufficiently.
- Hugging Mum or Dad, wanting to still hold hands, while out of the home; peers may see this and laugh; the individual may lack insight into the impact of this.
- Not dancing as well as others.
- Calling out too loudly – pragmatic dysfunction – not being able to recognise the need to modulate the voice, and sounding too loud or aggressive.
- Being too truthful, too honest – 'I don't like that dress, it makes you look fat'.
- Lacking flexibility in the interpretation of rules: 'He shouldn't do that – the teacher told us not to'.
- Emotional conflict – the realisation and frustration of being different and knowing that you are.
- Not seeing strengths, only weaknesses.
- Hooking on to disability rather than ability.
- Not giving good eye contact when talking to someone or being talked to.

Low self-esteem

The adolescent with DCD may feel increasingly alone as he or she lacks the skills of their peer group and acts emotionally younger than them. The gap is ever widening, their self-esteem sinking lower and lower.

Depression

The teenager may show a pattern of poor sleep, variable appetite, poor concentration, and feelings of low self-worth. This is often very difficult to detect, as many 'average' teenagers will show symptoms that could be seen as depressive, i.e. teenagers tend to sleep in, isolate themselves, are irritable and non-communicative for years! It is difficult to identify when there is true depression and not just normal teenage behaviour, and it is for this reason that many individuals may not be detected and treated properly.

Negative behaviour

This may start to emerge when the teenager feels a lack of support from school and home and may feel the need to act out in a more obvious way his or her sense of distress. This may be seen as negative behaviour both in school and at home, rather than at home only, which is the usual pattern for the younger DCD child. The teenager with DCD may not have yet been identified in the secondary school and the presentation of negative behaviour may be the only outward indicator and should cause alarm bells to ring in school if a previously well-behaved child starts to change their pattern of behaviour. Negative behaviour has been noted in other specific learning difficulties where social background, prenatal risk factors, birth weight, preschool language problems, and IQ have been excluded (Heiervang *et al.* 2001). It is likely that this is similar in the adolescent with DCD. It has been shown in studies that ADHD and DCD together appear to be a most important predictor of poor psychosocial functioning in early adulthood (Rasmussen and Gillberg 2000).

Lack the language of their peers

This is of enormous importance and is not always seen as a direct consequence of coordination difficulties. If the teenager lacks sporting skills, e.g. football, they are likely also not to be interested in being a spectator. The child does not watch football on television or follow a local team's progress, and if this is the case they are likely also to lack the language needed to join in conversation with peers. This leaves them further isolated.

Unfit and overweight

The teenager with DCD is already weaker at sport, and as most games in schools are team-based it will mean there are few opportunities for these teenagers to have the teaching to allow them to gain sufficient skills to join in and enjoy sport. This usually means a reluctance to try other sports and results in the teenager being less fit and more prone to putting on weight at this time. There is some evidence to suggest that physically active students perceive physical education classes more favourably than less physically active students (Anderssen 1993) and that parental and peer support for physical activity influences the individual to increase their activity levels. The findings indicate that, by serving as models and supporters, significant others have an important impact in promoting physical activity in young adolescents (Anderssen and Wold 1992). Larkin and Parker (1999) compared the responses of parents of 81 adolescents with DCD with those of a matched comparison group. While no significant differences were found in attitudes toward the benefits of physical activity, adolescents with DCD were involved in far fewer physical activities than their peers. This is an important message in secondary schools where sport often is not compulsory and if you do not have the requisite ball skills, 'joining in' becomes increasingly hard to do.

Appearance

Weight gain will make the teenager with DCD less attractive to the opposite sex. Their peers may also consider that he or she lacks good street credibility. The child may also be less aware of how to dress to be 'like' his or her peer group and because of lack of maturity, may not always see that this is how they are judged. In addition, there is resistance to being helped. Any suggestions regarding aids, equipment or tools only act to accentuate the fact that they are different from their peers.

Lack emotional maturity

Most teenagers with DCD, while being intellectually equal to their peers, often are emotionally younger by several years. They still require reassurance and support more in keeping with a child two to three years younger than their chronological age. This gap widens at this time and the years between 13 and 20 can be the hardest in the life of the individual with DCD trying to cope with all the changes that are occurring but lacking the maturity to take these changes on board. The ability to mix with younger children in primary school is now no longer an option when they move into secondary school.

> **Discussion** – What liaison has been set up between home and school to ensure good parent partnerships and how could this be improved? Do you have a resource area in school where parents can borrow information and also contribute information, e.g. let other parents know of local support groups, etc.?

Difficulties within the school setting

> **Case history**
> Sam is 14 years old. He arrived at the Dyscovery Centre for an assessment with a 'rocky' history of being thrown out of his nursery when he was three years of age and having difficult and negative behaviour since then. He was currently receiving a statement for his behaviour.

When Sam came to the Centre he seemed a polite and quiet boy. He was willing to be tested and to talk. All through his tests he asked the therapists how he was doing and was he getting it right. He wanted to know, and it seemed important to him to have feedback.

From his overall results it was clear that Sam had severe dyslexia with a reading age of around 5–6, little ability to write because of perceptual difficulties and poor coordination. He also had pragmatic language difficulties, which made it hard for Sam to be flexible and adaptable in differing situations and made his behaviour worse when he could not understand the lessons. In English he had been separated from the rest of the class, as he was disruptive. However he was probably only able to access about 20 per cent of the lesson because of his learning difficulties.

How did this child get so far in his education and not be recognised with such a difficulty?

(His father is also severely dyslexic but managed to become a successful professional. He had a childhood history of being moved from school to school to try and help him with his difficulties!)

What is different about secondary school?
The following differences can manifest themselves relating to secondary school:

- lack of key foundation study skills
- classes may be larger
- bigger school environment
- no personal desks and the use of lockers to store belongings
- subject-specific teachers
- independent travel to school
- homework – greater volume and expectation
- poor time concepts in an environment that demands performance in a time frame
- poor organisational skills when these need to be acquired to work independently
- lunch – coping with packed lunches or a canteen
- examinations to pass at a set time – determined by others
- career choices at a time when the child may not see he or she has any strengths
- An expectation that foundation skills are in place – secondary school usually means a faster pace. There are examinations to prepare for and results to attain. This means that in class there is no longer handwriting practice but the need to take notes down at speed with accuracy and legibility. If writing skills are poor this will have an impact on the individual when they come to review their work and may be unable to read their own writing. This means their notes may have little value when it comes to revision and examinations. They then have to work harder gaining that information when revising and may end up having to rely solely on textbooks.

They may also have auditory memory and processing difficulties which mean that they may miss out on information given to them in class – seemingly hearing the first bit and the last piece of a story but missing the middle. This ends up with the child not being able to access the lesson fully and they again have to catch up at home, working twice as hard to keep up with peers.

A level of literacy is seen as a prerequisite, but is not always assessed to ensure that it is present. The child may also have weak mathematical skills and not have the foundation skills in place to move on to more complex mathematics.

- Larger class sizes than primary school can leave the individual lost at the back of the class. Many children will either adopt a 'class clown' approach, or withdraw and be forgotten as they make little attempt to interact in the class. If they do try to do so and ask for help and repetition of information that has already been given, then this may be viewed as them being lazy and inattentive, and not be picked up as a sign that they may not have fully understood.
- Larger school environment can be bewildering. The child with DCD often has a poor sense of direction and will get lost in a new environment. They may not recognise the blank walls, and the different buildings may look all the same. The child has to negotiate from one site to another in less time, as well as carrying all his or her possessions around.
- No desks or lockers – some children will be required to carry around their possessions and books with them all day. For the child with DCD it can be extremely difficult to organise books and papers, and not lose equipment. Folders and papers become scrunched up at the bottom of the bag. The locker itself may present a difficulty if it has a small key to use. This may be difficult for the child and they may end up losing key after key. Others may take this as not caring, rather than seeing the organisational difficulties.
- Subject-specific teachers – not all the teachers may have knowledge of the child's difficulties and they may lack expertise in DCD. This has an impact on how the delivery of lessons needs to be adapted to allow the child to access the curriculum. Risk assessment may be needed, e.g. in Chemistry or Cookery. The teacher is under pressure to get through a packed curriculum with little disruption and has clear hurdles to overcome. A more complex child may present real difficulty when there are 29 or more other children to consider.
- Independent travel – the child may now need to travel to school independently and negotiate crossings, public transport, and have to manage money, increasing the stress levels prior to arriving at school each day.
- Homework – this may be the first time that the child has additional work set at the end of the day. Catch-up may also be required. For most children with DCD, fatigue is something they live with. Every day means a huge effort to concentrate and produce work. By the end of the day the child is usually exhausted and may be less productive. They may also have not been able to take down the homework, as the class may have been noisy and that made it

harder for them to hear as well as write the information down. They may also have put the wrong books in their bag. This will compound anxiety when they go home, knowing that the next day they will get into trouble for failing to do the homework.

- Time concepts – the inner clock does not seem to tick in the same way for children with DCD, or tick at all. The child does not usually seem to be aware of time passing. However, at the adolescent stage it is vital that the child understands the meaning of time as they have to, for example, complete examinations, be able to plan and organise their time appropriately, and be aware of when they are halfway through a test. This now becomes a big problem for many secondary school children with DCD, and remains so for many into adulthood. It becomes a problem getting to places on time, as well as completing tasks in time.

  It has been noticed that many individuals with DCD often do not seem to bother to wear a watch, and this may be because it does not seem to have any relevance to them. Most people tend to look at their watches to confirm the time. We have an inner clock that tells us that it is about the right time to go, or do something. The child with DCD does not seem to have this, so requires an external reminder of the time such as using alarms and buzzers. Alternatively they may require techniques to build up a 'feeling' of what time means, such as learning what 5 minutes is, or build up an awareness of regular trips, e.g the 20-minute car journey to school each day.

- Organisational skills – this also becomes more of an issue as the child is now supposed to be a more independent learner. They need to plan and organise the writing of essays and to organise their work so that they can find what they want at a later date, for example. These skills are usually particularly weak.

- Lunch – usually canteen style rather than a formal lunch setting. This requires the child to negotiate their lunch meal on a tray with a cup full of liquid placed on it. This is difficult to do at the best of times but made much worse when others are jostling for position. They may choose something less nutritious but easier to handle.

- SATs and GCSEs on the horizon – these now put greater pressure on the child, from their family and the school. There are greater opportunities to compare their ability, or lack of it, against others. They may not be emotionally ready to be put under pressure at this stage and may be being set up to fail, further reinforcing their negative feelings.

- Time to have to make career choices – at a time when the individual may not yet have decided who he or she is and what their skills are. For many teenagers this is hard enough. The child with DCD is yet to see whether they have any strengths at all, and may only be able to see the difficulties.

Discussion – Consider the following in relation to the school you are currently working in, or from past experiences:

What equipment may the individual require?

What social support could you put in to help?

What adaptations to lessons could be given to make them more inclusive?

What provision is there at breaktimes and lunchtimes to help the child?

Is there any provision for a safe quiet area for the child to withdraw to if required?

What adaptations would you consider are required for the classroom?

Discussion – Examination support

What time allowances should be made for children with DCD and should extra resources such as amanuensis be provided?

Consider how you would assess a child's needs for extra help in examinations.

Have you considered practice time to be given to children with an amanuensis, so that the child can be given the chance to learn this particular skill?

Does extra time in examinations always answer the problems for the child with DCD?

What subjects are harder for the individual with DCD?

Could and should considerations be made in the curriculum and exemptions be made for some subjects?

Which subjects would you consider harder to study and why?

A Dyspraxia/DCD Policy for your School
What are the 5 Key Areas you would consider?

1.

2.

3.

4.

5.

Difficulty	Changing the individual	Changing the environment
Examinations – finishing in time		
Writing		
Lectures		
Essays		
Homework		
Science lessons		
Disorganised		
Poor time management		
Untidiness		
Mathematics		
Cookery		
PE and Games activities		

Difficulty	Changing the individual	Changing the environment
Examinations – finishing in time	**Use of timer**	**Extra time** Being told when extra time starts, clock in room easily visible
Writing	**Gaining keyboard skills** Gaining permission to use in examinations	**Amanuensis or a prompter to tell the time**
Lectures	**Learning to mind map**	**Provision of tape recorder** Notes from class Carbon copy of student's notes
Essays	**Learn study skills**	**Provide template** Teach study skills Time framework
Homework	Homework book to record work from home to school and back and/or small voice recorder attached to uniform so easily available	**Continue to record homework and check books into bag** Work on timetable
Science lessons	**Work in a group** Understand limitations and risks	**Allow to observe rather than carry out experiments** Do risk assessment Allow the child to stand rather than sit Provide adapted tools
Disorganised	**To-do lists** Voice recorder Clear pencil case with list attached	**Mentor or buddy to help organise** Assistance from LSA with planning and organising self and workspace
Poor time management	**Watch with buzzer alarm** Timers Planner for everyday and for homework	**Assistance with scheduling**
Untidiness	Repeating and learning skills to become automatic	Help with colour coding of files, poly-pockets for notes, colour-coded disks for computer, setting up a system for the student
Mathematics	Understanding abstract concepts – there is a need to use kinaesthetic and visual methods	Introduce IT and visual programmes such as 'Numicon' where the individual can see what an increase in size means for example
Cookery	Have recipes photocopied to follow and tick off	Make sure the tools are appropriate, e.g. use Dycem under bowls and rubber handled knives, butter board for spreading
PE and Games activities	Ensure clothes are adapted if necessary so that the individual can make a quick change	Look at basic ball skills. Build up shoulder and hip stability; use exercises that the whole class can do Work on stamina training Be aware that understanding directions and moving is hard to do

Transition 'tick list' from secondary school to further education

1. Careers advice has to take into consideration skills as well as deficits.

2. What help will be required in college?

3. Start early with independent living skills – can the individual make a snack, self-care, organise his/her clothes and his/her bedroom?

4. Can he/she manage money, use public transport, and go shopping? – if not, these need to be taught prior to leaving home to ensure confidence and ability.

5. Is the individual organised in his/her work? Can he/she plan and produce course work on time and legibly? What skills does he/she need to learn now so as to ensure he/she will be able to do this at college?

6. Does the individual need help with classroom ergonomics: where he/she is seated; is the aisle too busy and distracting; how he/she is seated; are the chair and table too high or too low; what tools has he/she to complete a task; does all this need to be considered in a good transition plan?

7. Will he/she require assistance with recording information in lectures – will this need to be a scribe, could he/she use a tape recorder, or will access to course notes be sufficient?

8. What level of assistance has he/she had so far for examinations – will this still be required if a laptop can be used, will he/she require an amanuensis (scribe for examinations)?

9. Will he/she require special supervision, specialised computer support?

10. Is he/she aware of time – does he/she need to learn what time means, e.g. halfway through an examination, extra time, time required to travel to a meeting?

11. What are his/her self-caring skills like? Can he/she wash own hair, shave, wipe bottom? Can she manage her periods appropriately?

12. What level of social skills exists? Will the individual find it hard to meet new people and ask for help when he/she arrives in a new environment? Can he/she ask for what he/she wants without it being misinterpreted or not understood?

13. Has the individual required any form of counselling or therapeutic support – will this need to be continued, and in what form?

14. Would the individual be better attending college: at home – living at home, living in a hall of residence, in home town – living independently with others or on their own, in nearby town within an hour's travel or further away, or living with relatives?

15. Does the individual have a mobile phone, means of contacting family easily, are there pre-programmed numbers in the phone for him/her to use?

The long-term implications of DCD

For individuals with mild to moderate DCD, the outcome into adulthood is good, as many will probably learn to compensate for their difficulties. However, 50 per cent of motor impaired children will still have motor difficulties (Cantell 1998).

Some individuals seem to benefit from their growth spurt, and this may be caused by the enhancement of maturation of parts of their central nervous system (Visser *et al.* 1998). Children with additional attention difficulties as well as coordination difficulties have also been seen to have more behavioural problems in adolescence (Hellgren *et al.* 1993).

The child with more severe difficulties is more likely to continue to have functional difficulties into adolescence and into adulthood (Cantell *et al.* 1994). There is some evidence that he or she may also be more likely to be held back a year or to have been placed in lower sets (Gueze and Berger 1993).

The individual is also likely to have lower academic ambitions. This may be related to poorer self-concept (Losse *et al.* 1991). This may affect the type of career choices the individual makes, as they perceive themselves less able than they may actually be. Skinner and Pick (2001) in their work showed that those individuals they studied with DCD were found to perceive themselves as less competent in several areas, and having less social support than the control group. Overall, DCD individuals had lower self-worth and higher levels of anxiety than the control groups. Adolescents also perceived themselves as less competent with poorer social support and lower self-worth than younger children. In addition, anxiety was significantly higher for the adolescent group compared to their younger counterparts. The long-term implications of chronic anxiety are that they could potentially lead to an increased risk of depression in adulthood (Fox and Lent 1996).

References

Anderssen, N. (1993) 'Perception of physical education classes among young adolescents: do physical education classes provide equal opportunities to all students?', *Health Education Research*, 8 (2), 167–79.

Anderssen, N. and Wold, B. (1992) 'Parental and peer influences on leisure-time physical activity in young adolescents', *Research Quarterly for Exercise and Sport*, 63 (4), 341–8.

Cantell, M. H. (1998) 'DCD in adolescence: perceptual motor, academic and social outcomes of early motor delay', *Research Reports on Sports and Health*, 112. LIKES: Research Centre for Sports and Health Science, Jyvaskyla, Finland.

Cantell, M. H., Smyth, M. M. and Ahonen, T. P. (1994) 'Clumsiness in adolescence: educational, motor, and social outcomes of motor delay detected at 5 years', *Adapted Physical Activity Quarterly*, 11, 115–29.

Fox, A. M. and Lent, B. (1996) 'Clumsy children. Primer on developmental coordination disorder', *Canadian Family Physician*, **42**, October, 1965–71.

Gillberg, I. C., Gillberg, C. and Groth, J. (1989) 'Children with preschool minor neurodevelopmental disorders, V: Neurodevelopmental profiles at age 13', *Developmental Medicine and Child Neurology*, **31**, 14–24.

Gueze, R. and Berger, H. (1993) 'Children who are clumsy. Five years later', *Adapted Physical Activity Quarterly*, **10**, 10–21.

Heiervang, E., Stevenson, J., Lund, A. and Hugdahl, K. (2001) 'Behaviour problems in children with dyslexia', *Nordic Journal of Psychiatry*, **55** (4), 251–6.

Hellgren, L., Gillberg, C., Gillberg, I. C. and Enerskog, I. (1993) 'Children with deficits in attention, motor control and perception (DAMP) almost grown up: general health at 16 years', *Developmental Medicine and Child Neurology*, **35**, 881–92.

Larkin, D. and Parker, H. E. (1999) 'Physical activity profiles of adolescents who have experienced motor learning difficulties'. 11th International Symposium for Adapted Physical Activity, Quebec, IFAPA International Federation of Adapted Physical Activities.

Losse, A., Henderson, S. E., Elliman, D., Hall, Kinght, E. and Jongmans, M. (1991) 'Clumsiness in children. Do they grow out of it? A 10-year follow up study', *Developmental Medicine and Child Neurology*, **33**, 55–68.

Nickse, R.S. (1990) 'Family and intergenerational literacy programs', Information Series No. 342, ERIC Clearing House on Adult Careers and Vocational Education (ED 327736), Columbus.

Rasmussen, P. and Gillberg, C. (2000) 'Natural outcome of ADHD with developmental coordination disorder at age 22 years: a controlled, longitudinal, community-based study', *American Academy of Child and Adolescence Psychiatry*, 2000, **39** (11), 1424–31.

Skinner, R. A. and Piek, J. P. (2001) 'Psychosocial implications of poor motor coordination in children and adolescents', *Human Movement Science* **20** (1–2), 73–94.

Visser, J., Geuze, R. H. and Kalverboer, A. F. (1998) 'The relationship between physical growth, level of activity and the development of motor skills in adolescence. Differences between children with DCD and controls', *Human Movement Science*, **17**, 573–608.

CHAPTER 7

The adult

Learning objectives
- To understand the key elements to consider in transition from secondary school to further education and into employment.
- To critically evaluate the requirements for aids and adaptations for further education and in employment.
- To critically evaluate the long-term social and psychological impact on an individual with DCD.

Learning outcomes
- To be able to construct an appropriate management plan so that home, college/ university/employment and the individual are considered.
- To advise about aids and adaptations for the adult in the workplace or at home.
- To consider who should be a part of the interdisciplinary team and how their roles may relate to one another and to the individual with DCD.

Adolescence to adulthood

Transition is a key problem at the different stages of moving from adolescence to adulthood. Key times are:

- From secondary school to further/higher education
- Leaving home and having independent living skills
- Gaining employment and staying in employment

The key issues for adults with DCD

Leaving the formal and structured education of school and having greater choices about further education may feel both liberating and scary. For many years the

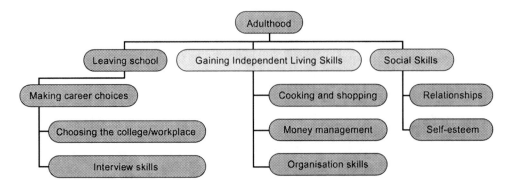

Figure 7.1   Key issues

individual may have felt like a round sausage in a square sausage machine, never quite fitting in. For the first time the individual can get rid of some of the barriers to effective learning and choose how they live and how they want to work. They no longer have to study subjects they have had great difficulty with. For example, there is no need to hand write if using a laptop is more efficient. He or she, and not others, can now dictate the style of clothes they wear and the way they conduct their life. There is less of a need to conform to the norm. This can be refreshing but also can cause concerns as now there are more choices to be made and less of a framework to follow. Change in the past may have caused stress and anxiety and this now may again be an issue in adapting and moving through this transition stage successfully.

Before moving on successfully there may be work that needs to be completed. Some adults may still want to seek the label that they never had, and dwell on this rather than addressing the functional difficulties that will lead to success or failure at college or in the workplace. The need for a label to give a meaning to the past and to acknowledge that the feelings the individual may have felt were real and founded in fact, is often an important issue. For many adults there may not have been recognition that the individual even had a specific learning difficulty, instead they may have been seen as stupid and clumsy. This may leave feelings of anger and frustration and a feeling of loss of 'self' through the school years and a consequential lack of progress made, because the individual did not see his or her true worth and ability.

For many, school days may have been the worst, and it is only after leaving school that there is the awakening of potential skills. However, for some, the low self-esteem and feelings of self-worth can also develop into depressive symptoms, and may require specialist treatment. Young people with DCD may become clinically depressed in adolescence and have been shown to be at significantly increased risk of later major depression, anxiety disorders, nicotine dependence, alcohol abuse or dependence, suicide attempts, educational underachievement, unemployment, and early parenthood. The associations noted in research undertaken were similar for both girls and boys. The results suggested the presence of two major pathways linking early depression to later outcomes. Research by Fergusson and Woodward (2002) suggests a direct linkage between early depression and increased risk of later major depression or anxiety disorders. Second, the associations between early depression and other outcomes were explained by the presence of confounding social, familial, and individual factors.

Focusing on feeling positive is essential for future success. The beginning of this is to put the past into perspective and realise that past times may have been bad but the clock can not be turned back. If this is not done, then the individual may seem to get stuck, dwelling on weaknesses in themselves and the way others treat him or her, rather than seeing that they have an opportunity to make their own way in life. Counselling may need to be considered, or the use of therapy such as cognitive behavioural therapy.

The degree of difficulty will vary enormously from one individual to another. Some of the areas of difficulty may be minor, such as tasks in the kitchen, whereas others such as socialising and sustaining friendships may remain problems that continue throughout adulthood. As DCD is often part of a co-morbid condition, each individual's needs are different and need to be assessed and met on that basis.

This chapter addresses generalities to cover all aspects that *may* occur, but do not always *all* occur. There is little research at present that looks at the long-term outcomes for adults with DCD and related difficulties. In the USA and Canada this group is sometimes known as 'non-verbal learning difficulties' and the same conclusions have been met, that concentrating on social skills as an outcome is of key importance (Dugbartey 2000).

However there are some general skills that we all need to acquire to be active and successful adults and these are usually the areas that most commonly remain a difficulty for the adult with DCD (see Figure 7.2). These skills are often the ones that are weakest and may not have been tackled in school, and require support and training to set up the right environment for success.

Successful transition from school into the workplace means that appropriate multidisciplinary working occurs between different agencies. There needs to be good transfer of information as well as ongoing interagency communication. Historically this has been poor, not just in supporting individuals with DCD but in more common areas requiring this type of provision, such as mental health services. It has not been without difficulties. The concept of trans-disciplinary working where there is client involvement is still very poor (Martin *et al.* 1999).

This concept of trans-disciplinary working where agencies work together with a primary worker may allow a better model of practice for the adult. This has been used with a project in South Wales, called the BOLD project (Borderline Learning

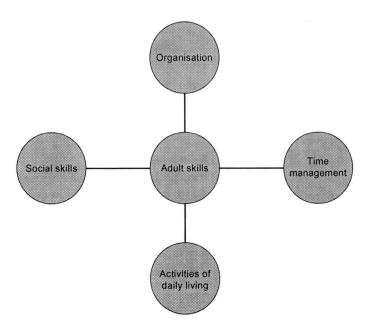

Figure 7.2   Areas of difficulty for the adult

Difficulties), where a key liaison person works with others on a consultancy basis to seek out the best management plan for the adult. Use of a share care organiser in this project has also allowed health, educational and social service information to be collated and held with the individual. The key worker system allows for transfer and collation of information to be done in a logical manner and reduces the need for several agencies to collect the same information. This has both time and cost implications for the client and the providers working with him or her.

There is still a great deal of work required in considering who needs to be a part of the support team and how interagency working can be most effective for the individual with DCD (Cook *et al.* 2001). There is a need to also consider what training needs to be undertaken by those individuals who will train adults with DCD. At the present time the level of knowledge is, at best, patchy. Greater understanding of the way the adult needs to learn is important – the time required to learn a new task and allowances that need to be made. Many adults with DCD can and will learn a new skill, but extra time needs to be given and the component parts for learning need to be shown. If skills in task analysis are not given to the trainer then the result is failure in the student. Some individuals with DCD, because of not seeing success academically, will end up in more practically focused training environments. The trainers in these institutions are likely not to have been trained in the field of specific learning difficulties even though, proportionately in their classes, more individuals than in the general population will have specific learning difficulties.

The individuals often fall through the gaps in services and find it harder to access help and support as they are often not seen as 'severe' enough. Their IQ often belies the difficulties they may be going through. Research by Murphy *et al.* (2002) with adults diagnosed with ADHD has shown a greater likelihood of alcohol dependence/abuse, cannabis dependence/abuse, as well as greater psychological distress. The ADHD groups studied were more likely to have received psychiatric medication and other mental health services than control adults. As the incidence of overlap between conditions is high, it is important to support and provide help for adults who may be at greater risk of mental health, and drug and alcohol difficulties.

> **Discussion** – Consider who should be a part of the interagency team for the adult with DCD and at what stage should this process begin. Critically analyse the difficulties that may occur among this group and consider potential ways of overcoming them.

Areas that remain difficult into adulthood

Many children with DCD will have grown up not having a clear view of what their strengths are. These have been children who seemed so surprised when told that they are able and bright. Their self-belief is so poor. The impact of years of low self-esteem for some means that the ability to approach adulthood with confidence is sometimes difficult.

This can have an effect in a number of ways, which do not appear to be related to the initial difficulties of poor coordination but are more consequences of it. Tying shoelaces and colouring-in are no longer issues. Playing ball sports and being a team player are no longer essential skills. Dyshockia is cured! (Not being able to play hockey!)

Social and psychological well-being
- Forming and sustaining relationships – making friends may have always been harder to do, and so without sufficient practice these skills may still be poor. This may be especially stressful when going into a new environment where there are no clear guidelines on what to expect and who to meet. Relationships may seem to be able to be made but are often hard to sustain. There may be a measure of not knowing the pace and speed to move at in a relationship, e.g. when it is appropriate to kiss, and touch, and get close. Previous failure leads to future anxiety.
- Mental health – individuals with more severe difficulties may show symptoms

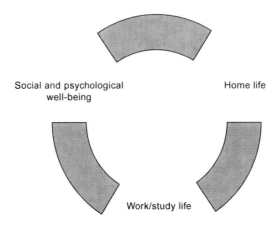

Social and psychological
well-being

Home life

Work/study life

Figure 7.3   Planning a cycle of success

of depression and feelings of chronic anxiety. Depression may present as low self-esteem, feelings of worthlessness, sleep disturbance, difficulty with concentrating and appetite disturbance. These symptoms should be treated in a traditional way using medication, or approaches such as cognitive behavioural therapy. It is not known if there is a direct link between DCD and depression but there may be similar root causes to both conditions. Interestingly, an Israeli group of researchers have shown the improvement of depression by taking omega-3 fatty acid supplementation. This could be tenuous evidence to support the link between the two disorders (Stoll *et al.* 2001).

- Body image – for many adults with DCD, their self-image may have been distorted. Poor kinaesthesia means that their self-perception may not be accurate. The individual may have been overweight for many years and only now be addressing the issue of caring for their body and improving how they look to others. Poor attitudes from others may have damaged his or her self-esteem over a long period.
- Persistence of negative behaviour – this may have been first seen in the adolescent with DCD and may escalate in some into increasingly negative social behaviour, ending up in being caught in the penal system. Studies have shown that there are a greater percentage of individuals with specific learning difficulties in the prison population than would be expected, some of whom have not been clearly identified in school days as having a specific learning difficulty (Rasmussen *et al.* 2001). A study in a Scottish prison showed the level of dyslexia was as high as 50 per cent (Kirk and Reid 2001). This is an effect of social drift, where there is a lower level of academic achievement and fewer chances of job success. This leads to a higher risk of antisocial behaviour.

Workplace/college
- Going to college or into the workplace – this may be extremely stressful and have a knock-on effect in other areas. Seemingly simple tasks, for example remembering details such as telephone numbers, may become a problem when under stress to perform. This can be enough for some adults to avoid going for interviews or to a new job because of past experiences. Often the first task asked of an adult in going into a job centre or applying for a job is to fill in a form. In the past this often had to be accompanied by a hand-written letter. The employer may misinterpret poor handwriting for poor skills, and the individual may miss out on a job that they are able and quali-fied to undertake.
- Writing a CV or completing an application form – this can cause problems in deciding what to disclose and how much. Too much detail could put off the employer or college; too little information could mean that the job or place at college is given inappropriately and, when the individual then arrives, it is apparent that he or she requires additional support. The individual has to decide what their past experiences have been and also the level of their present difficulties. They need to be realistic in deciding what level of support they may require. This may need external assistance to check whether percep-tion and reality match.

> **Discussion** – What level of assessment is done prior to employment or college to ascertain the baseline skills of the student and how will this relate to support needed while in university or in the workplace?

Employment
There are a number of areas relating to employment where additional support will be required:

- Starting a job or training – before even getting a job, interview techniques may need to be rehearsed. The individual will require a clear understanding of the processes that need to be undertaken through the day and the implied and explicit rules of the job.
- Continuing in employment – changes in a job may cause new difficulties for someone who is settled into the pattern of the job. The pattern of getting and not maintaining a job is one that is seen in individuals with DCD. Verbally very able and often intellectually able to cope with the job, the organisational difficulties may impact and cause breakdown.
- Gaining promotion – this is likely to mean that the individual has to gain a

new set of skills, e.g. IT skills, managerial/people skills, presentational skills. These may need to be formally taught and should not be assumed.

- Working together – attitudes to others and by others need to be explored. What do peers know about the individual's difficulties? How much will they make allowances when they still have to get on with the job themselves? This may be dependent on the pressure on the company to perform and the level of demand for the job when other people can jump into that position relatively easily.

- The 'Boss' – how understanding, flexible, and willing to be adaptable to different ways of delivering solutions to situations? What is his or her knowledge base? Individuals in a new job situation may not be adept at picking up the social hierarchies that may be in place, and not be sensitive to the differing behaviours of people they are working with. This can often cause early conflict where the adult with DCD may seem confrontational, this being without real intent.

- Organisational difficulties – these may show as a range of difficulties such as getting work assignments completed on time or organising the environment around the person. The individual's room may appear chaotic and this impacts on getting to work or to lectures on time. It may be harder to plan work, and it may end up often being finished at the last minute. This also has an impact on stress and anxiety levels. Even work completed may become lost. Of course many students without difficulties live like this, however for the individual with DCD this has a greater significant impact on his or her life.

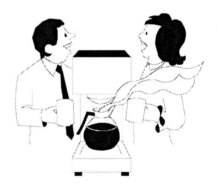

- Time management and planning – this can have an effect in many areas, for example, getting to an interview on time, leaving to catch a bus on time, leaving the house at the same time with others, or completing a task in time. This will then have an impact on relationships when other people do not understand why someone can find this such a problem, and can be a focal point in a relationship where someone else may be very punctual. This is an issue from early childhood where an inner concept of time passing remains a difficulty.

Discussion – What aids and adaptations could be put in place to help the adult with organisation and time management?

Home life
- In the kitchen – difficulties with tasks that others take for granted may occur from the moment of rising till the end of the day. There may be difficulty in following a recipe, slicing and buttering bread, using a tin-opener, or separating an egg. This is usually related to poor fine motor coordination and organisational difficulties.
- Dress codes – see Chapter 6.
- Shopping/making lists – organisational skills are often poor, and there may need to be visual prompts to remind the individual of tasks that need to be done and the order in which they need to be completed. Following a recipe may be difficult and may be helped by photocopying some recipes and ticking the ingredients off as the person undertakes the tasks, or teaching the individual three or four key recipes that can then be adapted.
- Travel – the types of difficulties may be catching the right bus, knowing which side of the road to catch it from, and being prepared with the correct amount of money for the fare. Past errors in dealing with this type of problem may increase future anxiety.
- Using money and managing a budget – this is also an organisational issue, and may require low-level intervention to ensure success in looking after finances. Putting systems in place initially can make a big difference to future management and reduce the risk of failure later on.
- Learning to drive – this may take much longer to learn as the individual is having to learn a number of skills and coordinate them at the same time. Use of simulated driving classes helps to acquire and automate some of the skills before getting out on to a real road. Use of an automatic car rather than manual to begin with is also a means of reducing the number of different tasks at any one time. The individual may find they have difficulties with right/left orientation, especially at speed or while taking oral instructions from someone else; visual perception, how near to a wall or when parking.

Physical difficulties
There is some evidence to show that coordination difficulties do remain for a proportion of individuals with DCD. Tasks requiring fine motor coordination such as threading a button, using a tin-opener, or cutting with a pair of scissors may remain difficult.

Gross motor difficulties such as playing sports may be less of a problem as the individual no longer has to be competitive and can participate for pleasure. He or she is not being measured against other people's performance.

Activities such as swimming, canoeing, badminton and hiking may cause fewer problems than team-based sports. Other sports may all be learnt but require persistence in gaining skills in the early stages. Activities like Tai Chi, Alexander

Technique, Pilates and yoga may be advantageous to take up to help with posture and flexibility.

Long-term implications of poor stability and adaptation may lead the adult to have tight 'hamstring' muscles and tight Achilles tendons. The adult may also have back pain because of years of adapting posture to cope with coordination difficulties. They may have had to cope with chronic back pain because of hypermobility of joints (Grahame 2000). This may have a psychological effect as well as a physical one. Even headaches caused by temperomandibular dysfunction may be occurring where there has been ligamentous laxity around the jaw.

Discussion – Consider and critically analyse the processes that could be put in place for an individual with DCD leaving school and moving into

(a) further education
(b) employment.

Consider what professionals should be a part of a transition plan and how they should interface with one another successfully.
   Reflect on current practice and what the barriers for success are.
   Consider what current service provision exists in your area, and nationally, and consider how this could be better utilised in the future.
   Compile a list of resources in your area that could be used with students to signpost them in the right direction for help, e.g MAVIS, DEA, careers services, voluntary sector.

Planning for the future and addressing difficulties

The individual with DCD may never have gone through a process of planning his or her future and is more likely to have failed in school than succeeded. Many of the successes the individual may have had are ones he or she has achieved outside of school. Interests and hobbies often become the basis of future training and employment.

Creating a plan of action

The individual requires a need to consider the following.

Short-term goals

- What to avoid?

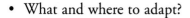

  - Unsuitable work situations. What is the best setting to work in, e.g. a small office with a discrete work area?
  - Type of work that will cause difficulties, e.g. working in an environment with a great deal of change.
  - Working in an environment where there is little direction.
  - Inflexible working hours or patterns that do not take into account fatigue or poor time management.

- What and where to adapt?

  - The home environment, e.g. organising the bedroom and clothes, bathroom and shower, adaptations.
  - The kitchen – adapted tools, e.g. tin-opener, bread spreader, recipes, shopping.
  - The work environment, e.g. risk assessment in chosen career, ergonomics of the workplace, seating, tools to be adapted (knives in a kitchen, office equipment, use of a keyboard).

- What skills still need to be improved?

  - Social skills, e.g. learning to be in a new environment.
  - Learning how and when to modulate the voice.
  - Learning how to organise self and improving time management skills.
  - Learning how to be realistic about the goals that are being set, and how many steps are required to see success.
  - Learning keyboard skills to avoid having to write.
  - Positive thinking skills.

- What are the strengths/weaknesses of the individual?

  - The individual needs to see what he or she is good at, e.g. kind and caring, creative.
  - The need to be realistic about self-skills – this may be too high or too low.
  - Motivation and concentration may be low and there may be a need to learn to recognise the strengths that are actually there. Cognitive behaviour

therapy may be a useful approach in adults with DCD and has been used successfully in children with DCD (Missiuna *et al.* 2001).
  o Need to build up a positive picture – create a series of affirmations and repeat them until they become entrenched.

- What is the preferred learning style?

  o What does the individual prefer to do to learn, e.g. listen to instructions or read instructions?

Long-term goals
- Realistic goals – becoming an astronaut or rugby player may be hard for the individual with DCD, but aspirations that relate to intelligence rather than past experience need to be discussed so that the individual sees what options may be available.
- How long is a long-term goal – one year, five years, ten years? Does this need to be discussed with the individual and then put in writing?
- What does he or she want in both their personal and professional life and how can they change their short- and medium-term goals to achieve it?
- What barriers does he or she see and are they real?

The adult in the workplace/university

Choosing a job
How should this be done and what help does the individual require? There is often a need to have some support in matching skills to the job and setting up the job scene for success. By informing the employer of potential difficulties and planning in advance, many of the problems can be minimised. This may be as simple as making sure that all instructions for work need to be written down and the individual needs to compile a 'to do' list to see where he or she is in the process. The next stage is ensuring the individual is ready for employment and has the skills that are required, such as social interaction and listening skills. A job taster is one way of the employer and employee trying out several different types of workplace without added pressure.

Risk assessment is essential, for example in working in a kitchen where should the person stand or sit, does he or she require special knives for food preparation, is speed of preparation an issue?

Choosing a university/college
It is important to consider an action plan for transition.

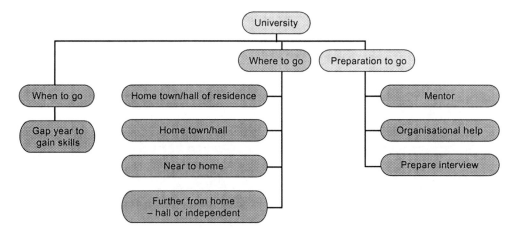

Figure 7.4 Factors relating to going to university/college

- When to go?
  - Is this the right time to go on to higher education or should the individual consider a number of stepping-stones to ensure success?
  - Is the individual emotionally mature enough to cope with a new course, new town, the new environment of a university, new friends and new lecturers, or should it be delayed until appropriate provision is put in place to increase the chances of success?
  - What particular tools are needed to set up the individual for success, either in the course or at home, e.g. in planning and preparing meals, and shopping?
  - Has the Disability Students Allowance been applied for?
- Where to go?
  - Is it better to consider a home town college or to move away?
  - The home town is more familiar. If the individual wants to go away, is there a good rail/road service so that they can come home easily if they want to?
  - Does the university or college have special needs support and is the proposed course 'do-able'?
  - What amount of realistic and appropriate support needs to be put in place, for example asking for notes for the course, alternative note-taking, and a laptop computer with mind mapping on it (if this is seen to be helpful)?
  - Is it better for the individual to live independently or to live at home where there will still be greater support, or is the hall of residence with ready prepared meals a halfway house?
- What preparation? Before starting in an unfamiliar town it is worth pre-planning for difficulties and visiting on several occasions.

- ○ Find out where local shops are situated.
- ○ What is the transport system and is a bus pass useful?
- ○ Getting to know the way around the campus. Is a map available?
- ○ Going through all the potential problems will allow the individual to be prepared on the first day, as the individual with DCD is already disadvantaged.

- If the individual aims to live independently, can he or she:

  - ○ Plan, shop, prepare a meal and clean up afterwards?
  - ○ Self-care – wash themselves, wash their clothes and use an iron? If they are not able to, what provision is there for help?

- Preparation of required skills
  - ○ Organisational skills often need to be taught and put in place. Once there, they also may need to be reviewed to ensure that they are successful, e.g. a pegboard with notices, timetable of the week, filing system for course notes, bookshelf for books, baskets for clothes, shopping list of regular items, a weekly meal planner, colour-coded files and filing trays, polypockets in which to put bills to pay.
  - ○ A mentor may be required to put this in place and review it with the individual on a regular basis.

Applying for a job
The application
There is a need to match qualifications and experience to increase the chances of success. It will be harder to have a job that requires fast production times, e.g. in a fast food joint, or a job that requires multi-tasking, e.g. answering the phone, taking down information at speed.

Is the job too long and too hard? Adults with DCD often tire more easily and may find part-time working more successful to start with. Is there a potential for flexitime so that the individual can choose his or her hours, although this may cause problems if time management is an issue?

The interview
The individual should have prepared and rehearsed some questions and answers.

Discussion – What interview techniques are currently taught in school in preparation for employment or college? Is there an understanding that the individual may have difficulties with pragmatic language and so may not pick up on the subtle beginnings and endings of the interview that may be more non-verbal than verbal?

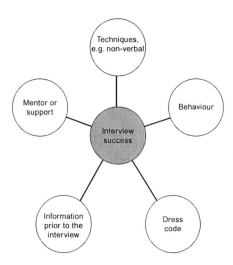

Figure 7.5   Attending a job interview

Discussion – Consider what you would include in a 'tool kit' for an interview to ensure the individual is prepared from the moment he or she leaves home until the end of the interview.

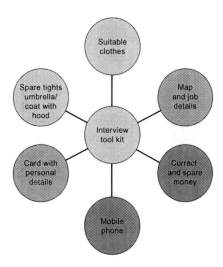

Figure 7.6   Going to an interview

Discussion – Adaptation and assistance by the employer.
What help may be required?

- Do physical changes need to be made to the environment where the individual is working?
- Who needs to be told and what and when do they need to be told?
- Does the person need to have additional tools? Who will assess requirements and provide them?
- Who will provide extra help and for how long should this be provided?
- What sources of funding are available in your area to support the individual in the workplace?
- Is there a need for workplace 'tasters' and how could this be structured to be successful?
- What knowledge does the employer/college have about DCD?
- What support services currently exist for individuals with DCD?

Creating a template for a student/employee to assess their needs

Key areas to consider	Environment	Skills base/deficit	Tools to help
Task Profile e.g. Using a computer	Where is it placed	Poor speed	Voice activated software
Travel to and from work			
Other areas such as entrances/ lockers			
Understanding of processes and rules			
Peer and employer interaction			

Breaks/hours of work			
Money management			
Health and safety legislation			
Access to the building			
Access to work-adaptations			
Organisational strategies required	Filing tray in work Workplace mentor to create work plan	Poor time keeping Loses paper Late for meetings Difficulty processing work	Palmpilot Corkboard with timetable Use of to do list to tick off as completed

Foundation for Success

Staying in the job
Adapting to change
Living independently
Maintaining relationships

Starting a job
Learning the day, learning the rules
Making new friends
Learning the job
Travel to the job

Time management
Planning a job
Needing specialised or adapted equipment

Interview techniques
Application forms
Disclosure
Attending training courses
Tool kit for interview

Home
Environment
Organisation
Getting up, dressing appropriately
Making a snack
Planning a day

Skills
Managing money
Using public transport
Navigating new environments
DIY/computer
Shopping and planning

Psychosocial
Social skills
Judgement
Self-esteem
Maturity
Sexuality
Making a relationship with same and opposite sex

Key learning points
- Organisational skills are a key to success.
- Social skills need to be worked on.
- Good forward planning increases chances of success.
- There is little research into the long-term outlook for adults, and this needs to be addressed by further research.

References

Cook, G., Gerrish, K. and Clarke, C. (2001) 'Decision-making in teams: issues arising from two UK evaluations', *Journal of Interprofessional Care*, **15** (2), 141–51.

Dugbartey, A. T. (2000) 'Nonverbal learning disability: adult outcomes', *Seminars in Clinical Neuropsychiatry*, **5** (3), 198–204.

Fergusson, D. M. and Woodward, L. (2002) 'Mental health, educational and social role outcomes of adolescents with depression', *Journal of Archives of General Psychiatry*, **59** (3), 225–31.

Grahame, R. (2000) 'Heritable disorders of connective tissue', *Practical Research in Clinical Rheumatology*, **14** (2), 345–61.

Kirk, J. and Reid, G. (2001) 'An examination of the relationship between dyslexia and offending in young people and the implications for the training system', *Dyslexia*, **7** (2), 77–84.

Martin, C. J., de Caestecker, L., Hunter, R., Gilloran, A., Allsobrook, D. and Jones, L. M. (1999) 'Developing community mental health services: an evaluation of Glasgow's mental health resource centres', *Health and Social Care in the Community*, **7** (1), 51–60.

Missiuna, C., Mandich, A. D., Polatajko, H. J. and Malloy-Miller, T. (2001) 'Cognitive orientation to daily occupational performance (CO-OP): Part I – theoretical foundations', *Physical Occupational Therapy in Paediatrics* **20** (2–3), 69–81.

Murphy, K. R., Barkley, R. A. and Bush, T. J. (2002) 'Young adults with attention deficit hyperactivity disorder: subtype differences in comorbidity, educational, and clinical history', *Journal of Nervous and Mental Disorders*, **190** (3), 147–57.

Rasmussen, K., Almvik, R. and Levander, S. J. (2001) 'Attention deficit hyperactivity disorder, reading disability, and personality disorders in a prison population', *American Academy of Psychiatry and the Law*, **29** (2), 186–93.

Stoll, A. L., Damico, K. E., Daly, B. P., Severus, W. E. and Marangell, L. B. (2001) 'Methodological considerations in clinical studies of omega 3 fatty acids in major depression and bipolar disorder', *World Review of Nutrition and Dietectics*, **88**, 58–67.

CHAPTER 8

Language and communication

Learning objectives
- Consider normal language development and variations from the norm and how these relate to communication before school and in school.
- Consider the implications of language in the context of the individual with DCD.

Learning outcomes
- Critically consider how this may impact on the delivery of information to children in the class.
- Consider the overlap of other conditions such as Asperger's on the child with DCD.

Introduction

Social and communication difficulties are a consistent feature of individuals with DCD. It is uncertain whether the motor difficulties affect communication or vice versa, although there does seem to be a link between the two. Could experiences of lower tone in babies with DCD mean that gaining and maintaining good eye contact with their mother is harder, and this means their ability to recognise facial expressions may be marred at an early and crucial developmental stage? Could this then have a knock-on effect on picking up non-verbal cues when older?

Certainly the tone and posture of an individual with DCD is often poor and the ability to gain and maintain good eye contact is harder. The slouching walk and slumped position in the child and adult also make others consider the individual to be less sociable. A 'sloppy' handshake at an interview and little eye contact makes others think the individual does not care about the outcome, which may be far from the truth. So posture affects the ability to communicate.

The other factor that we see in the individual with DCD is that they seem to have poor body awareness; not knowing where their body is in space. This has an impact on understanding social distance and may lead to the individual standing too close or too far away and not being able to judge appropriate social distance.

The incidence of *pragmatic dysfunction* (which includes non-verbal language) certainly seems more common than in the general population and this has an impact from early days on making and sustaining friendships. This has been attributed in the past to a sign of Asperger's Syndrome (which is also known as a part of the Autistic Spectrum Disorders (ASD)). The individual with DCD does seem to have pragmatic language difficulties (see later in the chapter for further explanation), but usually wants to be sociable but is 'clumsy' in the approach. The 'all or nothing' way of moving seems also to be seen in social interaction. The child also seems to mind if he or she does not get it right with their peers.

Early 'glue ear' – effect on language in children with DCD

At one stage it was thought there might be a link between early glue ear, also known as otitis media, and later language difficulties. However there is insufficient evidence to support attempts at early detection of glue ear in the first four years of life in the asymptomatic child to prevent delayed language development.

It is necessary to understand the normal developmental stages of language and communication to see a variation from the norm. The teacher then needs to identify key traits that may be picked up in the class while teaching, or in the playground, that may make him or her suspect a difficulty. (See Chapter 3 on stages of development and you can see where language and play 'fit in' alongside motor development.)

Non-verbal language

Non-verbal language is a difficulty in the following areas:

- Gestures and postures: What does a hand movement mean, or the way we sit with our arms crossed when talking to someone? Hand and arm movements that communicate meaning are called gestures; positions of the entire body that convey meaning are called postures. Both can convey messages that conflict with spoken words, confusing communication efforts.
- Person space: Can you recognise the unwritten space rules such as: up to 18 inches for personal space; 18 inches to 4 feet for interactive space; 4 to 12 feet for social space; and 12 feet and beyond for public space? We all carry portable territory and boundaries around with us. If you stand too close to others while having a conversation you are violating the rules of personal space; or if you touch someone inappropriately either in terms of location or intensity of that contact, this is breaking one of the unwritten laws of touch and you stand an excellent chance of being rejected without knowing why.
- Rhythm: What is the person's rate of walking, talking, eating, etc.? Speech

patterns, attitudes and the speed of movement or speech all fall into this category. A child from France has a different 'rhythm' from that of a child from New York. Their speech patterns and attitudes are indicative of the differences in their environments. Problems arise when they are out of 'sync' with one another. This also includes habits of time management, like arriving promptly or being late for appointments.

- Touch: What are the rules for touching another person and how may they be different from culture to culture?
- Faces: Recognising expressions on a face based on emotions of joy, anger, fear, sadness, etc.
- Paralanguage or Prosody: What does the tone of voice tell you?
- Objectics: Personal hygiene and style of dressing indicate that individuals are part of a group, and keep them from being singled out as strange or different. People frequently judge how you look first, before what you say, and if you are like or unlike themselves.

Difficulties seen in DCD

Children with DCD may be seen to play alongside and not interact with their peers. The turn-taking behaviour which is usually seen by the age of five years may not be reached even at 10 or 11 years, and a sign of this may be where the child still wants to lead a situation rather than follow. This is often a sign that the child needs to be in control; otherwise he or she may exhibit increased anxiety not knowing how it will be 'played out'.

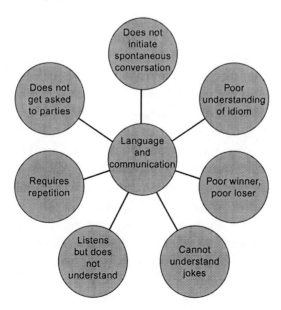

Figure 8.1 Difficulties seen in children with DCD

The DCD child is often very poor at both winning and losing and may seem to go 'overboard' with his or her behaviour. The child is like a car without social gears, being either all or nothing. They may end a game abruptly and walk off seemingly oblivious to others around them. The child may lack experience of 'good' endings in social play. Their past experiences are often abrupt and they may find it hard to persist to the end of the game when they realise they are losing.

Pragmatic language impairment
This is the inability to use communication skills appropriate to the situation. This leads to the following:

- Inability to decode non-verbal language, e.g. recognition of facial expressions, hearing tone in someone's voice, seeing gestures and understanding their meanings.
- Difficulty making judgements about the current situation based on previous situations – they seem to be less flexible and adaptable.
- Difficulty in predicting what would be appropriate in content and form.
- Difficulty in repairing any breakdown. This is often why the child leaves a situation completely as he or she lacks the strategies to make it better again. They feel anxious and remove themselves.

This results in:

- A lack of ability to generalise concepts to different objects and situations.
- Inability to do so – rigid word boundaries.
- Over-adherence to what is right (i.e. seeing things in black and white terms); this may be to the detriment of friendships, not understanding that if they 'tell' on a friend, their peers could potentially alienate them.
- Difficulty in recognising emotions in self and others. This may mean that the child only seems to react to 'big stuff', i.e. when someone shouts at the child or raises their hand, as the child finds it harder to pick up the earlier signs that the other person is unhappy.
- Literal understanding, e.g. 'you should never run in the corridor' – and not seeing that in an emergency you may have to.
- Problems with metaphor, idiom, sarcasm, e.g. it's raining cats and dogs, turn over, try harder, pick yourself up, pull your socks up.
- Sarcasm is important, in that it is frequently used in social conversation in secondary school and lack of understanding when and how it is used may make peer interaction even worse at this stage, especially where the main way to communicate is through 'grunts' and shrugs of the shoulders!

Discussion – Have you seen this type of behaviour in school in any of the children you have observed?

What help could be put in place to help the child and their peers to cope better and not to misinterpret the child's or their peers' behaviour?

How could the vulnerable child be 'protected' from their peers while they are learning skills and trying them out?

What social skill training is provided in schools and how could you put a plan of action in place to bring this into the school curriculum – what ways could this be introduced as a 'whole school' activity?

Could children be given social skills training in small mixed groups?

Draw up a profile of strengths and weaknesses of a child that you are concerned about in your class.

Skill	Key indicators	Observe
Basic conversation skills	Able to answer questions in appropriate time Able to initiate a conversation appropriately timed	
Tone and quality of speech	Volume appropriate Use varied tone in speech Rate appropriate	
Recognise others' emotions	Facial expression Gestures Posture	
Non-verbal skills	Recognise others' facial expressions Social distance – eye and body contact Gestures – appropriate and inappropriate – overuse of hugging, not shaking hands in a formal situation	
Ability to listen	Reflection, e.g. 'ums' and 'ahs' Question feedback through conversation Sharing with others Initiating two-way conversation – asking for comment – pausing for response	
Assertiveness	Expressing feelings Requesting explanation Refusing Apologising	

It is also always important to consider the other difficulties that coexist with DCD or may be a part of the same continuum. The child with DCD seems to be a child who wants to make friends and initiate play but does not have the skills to do it, but at the more severe end of the scale with Asperger's Syndrome, the child does not mind in the same way if they make social contact, and seems to mind less about the impact of their behaviour on others.

Asperger's Syndrome

Asperger's Syndrome (or Asperger's Disorder) is a neurobiological disorder named after the Viennese physician, Hans Asperger. It is often known as an Autistic Spectrum Disorder (ASD).

Hans Asperger described a pattern of behaviours in several young boys who had normal intelligence and language development, but who also exhibited autistic-like behaviours and marked deficiencies in social and communication skills.

Incidence
- Autism occurs in 4.5 per 10,000 people;
- Asperger's Syndrome occurs in approximately 26 per 10,000 people.

Signs and symptoms
- Individuals with Asperger's Syndrome (AS) can exhibit a variety of characteristics and the disorder can range from mild to severe.
- They may show marked deficiencies in social skills, have difficulties with transitions or changes and prefer sameness.
- They often have obsessive routines and may be preoccupied with a particular subject of interest.
- They have a great deal of difficulty reading non-verbal cues (body language) and very often the individual with AS has difficulty determining proper body space.
- Often overly sensitive to sounds, tastes, smells and sights, the person with AS may prefer soft clothing, certain foods, and be bothered by sounds or lights no one else seems to hear or see. It is important to remember that the person with AS perceives the world very differently.
- By definition, those with AS have a normal IQ and many individuals (although not all) exhibit exceptional skill or talent in a specific area.
- Vocabularies may seem advanced for their age but they may not actually be able to hold a good conversation with someone else in a two-way fashion.
- Persons with AS can be extremely literal and have difficulty using language in a social context.

How does the child present in school?
The following might be observed:

- needing to ask for instructions to be repeated;
- difficulty carrying out sequential instructions;
- missing and then guessing information given to them;
- adaptive strategies to hide their difficulties;
- word-finding difficulties – context bound;
- slow, hesitant or delayed output;
- excess use of words and speech with little or no insight into the impact on others;
- pedantic language – this may sound rather formal in structure – with abnormal prosody (intonation and rhythm) and may sound rather 'flat' and lack feeling.

The following non-verbal aspects might be seen:

- they are often bullied as they are not able to socialise easily with peers;
- not able to pick up facial and body cues and gestures;
- they may find that they are poor at judging social distance and stand too close or give too much eye contact;
- organisational difficulties;
- not understand idiom, sarcasm, metaphor.

The ASD child may also have difficulty with:

- slow auditory processing – as the child cannot keep up with the speed of information needing to be processed;
- perceptual gaps – they may seem to have gaps in understanding;
- lack of insight that they are missing information;
- misinterpretation of situations.

Help with language and communication difficulties
How can children with language and communication difficulties be helped in the school setting? The following general guidance is given:

- Understanding of the underlying difficulties of the child – this can then mean that the teacher does not make inappropriate judgements *why* the child is behaving in a certain way.
- Recognising where the difficulties lie in a social skills framework – witnessing the following behaviours may alert you to further analysis of the child's difficulties: difficulty in initiating and maintaining friendships, having difficult playtime with peers, bullying, difficulty initiating a conversation, being unable to pick up others' emotions, not being able to cope with change,

inappropriate personal comments to others, abruptly leaving a group. Each of these skills need to be taught in a group session where the child can practise the skills so that they become automated, even under pressure.

- Recognising the signs in the class or playground – e.g. in PE, walking alone in the playground, lack of Christmas cards or not being asked to parties, not wanting to be sat next to in class, misunderstanding rules, inappropriate laughter or other behaviour out of context for the situation.
- The need for a structure and framework – to allow the child to know what is happening and when. This needs to be in both a visual and verbal format.
- Indication in school of both implicit and explicit rules – and a discussion of how these may vary from time to time; also linked to home so that there is consistency for the child.
- Allowing 'time out' – if the child is feeling pressured or anxious.
- Discussing changing situations early – to prepare the child so he or she knows what to expect.
- Asking the child where he or she sees their social difficulties lying – e.g. not being asked to parties, being excluded from teams, worried about reading in class, eating out in public, meeting new people, and then working from this point. Each situation may need to be practised, and then there will be a need to vary the situation and discuss how this affects the type of language and behaviour.
- Working on facial gestures – there are a number of commercial games using facial expressions to check that the child has understood. Pictures could be cut from magazines, the child then guessing emotions depicted in the pictures (with angry, happy, sad and frightened as starting points, for example).
- How assertive is the child? – do they need help with learning how to express their feelings: refusing, apologising, and requesting an explanation for something they have not understood? They may need to practise these skills so that they can recognise the difference between aggression and assertiveness, and how this affects posture and tone of voice.
- There is a need to help the child understand what being socially able means – do they know what aggression means and what it looks like? Do they know the difference between assertive and aggressive (lots of adults do not know this one!)? You could use video or photography to demonstrate the differences in social interaction to help the child to identify the different situations. Allow the child to watch television with the sound turned down – can they tell you how people are behaving without conversation being heard?

The following approaches might be helpful.

Traffic light system

RED – inappropriate behaviours – this is for verbal and non-verbal behaviour, e.g. swearing at a teacher, touching someone on the inside of an arm or leg.

AMBER – behaviour and language for certain social settings.

GREEN – safe language and behaviour for all occasions.

Bull's-eye approach

- Inner zone is the child
- Next zone – parents
- Next zone – close friends and family
- Peers
- Teachers
- Adult family friends
- Outermost zone – strangers

Using this model allows the child to see the differences in how they act in different social settings with different people as they move to the outer zones – fine to hug Mum but not a stranger, etc. It allows for discussion about the way language is used differently with different people and acquaintances.

Time out card

Could the child be given a 'time out' card that they can use if they are feeling stressed and need to have five minutes in the quiet room in the school to 'cool' down and gain control once again? It may subtly alert the teacher that the child does not understand a situation but may not have the skills to verbalise it.

Other resources you might be able to use to help the child are outlined below.

- Wendy Rinaldi – Social Use of Language Programme (SULP). Helps to enhance the communication skills of children and adolescents with mild to moderate learning difficulties. It can be used to assess a person's social communication skills, both verbal and non-verbal, and can be used to implement an educational therapy programme.
- TEACCH. Provides structure and organisation in the classroom or any other learning environment for a student's level of understanding and can help to

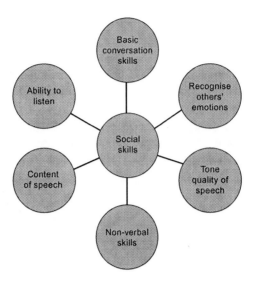

Figure 8.2   Caption to follow

alleviate or moderate these problems and the resultant ineffective learning situations. It uses a structured visual system to help provide organisation for the child.

- Social Stories – devised by Carol Gray. 'A social story is a story written according to specific guidelines to describe a situation in terms of relevant cues and common responses' (Gray and Garand 1993). The underlying philosophy stresses the importance of 'abandoning all assumptions' – to seek to understand the student's perspective, to ensure a student has the social information he or she needs, and to present information so it is accessible and easily understood. Social stories are often written for individual students, reflecting an understanding of a student's unique perception of a situation. However they require high levels of one-to-one time which may be difficult to give in a mainstream setting.
- Circle Time – developed by Jenny Mosley. This holds self-esteem building to be a central aim. The Quality Circle Time model provides a positive behaviour management system with a process of personal and social education.

Verbal dyspraxia

In considering language we need to also consider verbal dyspraxia. This is sometimes known as developmental verbal dyspraxia (DVD) and also known as apraxia of speech and as an oral motor planning disorder. It is not a muscle disorder. It is as if the brain is telling the muscles what to do and the messages are getting scrambled. There is nothing wrong with either end, but the signals cannot be translated properly.

How does it show itself?

It can show itself in the following ways:

- some children may have little or no babbling in infancy;
- their understanding of language seems better than their production;
- they may have slow or halting speech, and it sometimes appears to be a struggle to talk;
- they may be hard to understand;
- therapy is slow to improve the problem;
- individuals with DVD have difficulty with speech, especially at speed; they may avoid speaking, and therefore do not get the required practice.

What is wrong with the muscles?

The speech muscles are not paralysed. They just do not seem to work well together. Individuals with DVD may also have problems with non-speech tasks such as moving the tongue, puffing the cheeks, and opening and closing the jaw.

How is it recognised?

Children may have features of verbal dyspraxia, and also have associated generalised coordination difficulties. Some children may also have feeding problems. New sounds will take a time to learn, and they will have to concentrate hard to make that sound. They cannot always tell if their attempt at a sound is correct or not. They need a lot of practice before they can incorporate new sounds into syllables and words at a normal speed.

Treatment approaches

Achievements are slow and regular therapy over quite a long period of time may be required to make changes. The child needs to develop speech patterns and make them automatic.

Treatment has to start by looking at the child's oromotor skills – lip shaping, where the tongue is placed, and the ability of the lips and tongue to sequence movements. Non-cooperation may be a way of expressing difficulty. Older children may need to concentrate on concrete targets such as daily practice lists, and working to a set time limit, or the use of a scoring system so they can assess themselves and recognise signs of improvement.

Children with verbal dyspraxia will not grow out of it, and continuing work will need to be done over a period of time until full control is achieved. If appropriate help is not received, these children may be left with residual problems that may affect their educational progress, especially with writing and spelling.

References

Circle Time – Jenny Mosley Consultancies, 28A Gloucester Road, Trowbridge, Wiltshire BA14 0AA. Telephone: 01225 719204 Fax: 01225 755631. e-mail: *circletime@jennymosley.demon.co.uk*

Gray, C. and Garand, J. (1993) 'Social stories: improving responses of students with autism and accurate social information', *Focus on Autistic Behaviour*, **8** (1), 1–11.

Social Use of Language Programme (SULP) – Revised by Wendy Rinaldi. Windsor: NFER-Nelson.

TEACCH – see website at *http://www.teacch.com*

CHAPTER 9

Behaviour and psychosocial issues in DCD

Learning objectives
- To consider why children may exhibit behaviour that is seen as negative but which may have underlying reasons linked to specific learning difficulties.
- To critically consider current thinking around behaviour management and how this information may alter future management.
- What influences the behaviour of the child with DCD?
- To consider as professionals and parents how we usually respond to this behaviour.
- How can the child be helped?
- Critically analyse methods of behaviour management within your school and how they could be altered.

Learning outcomes
- To be able to put together a management plan for a child with behaviour difficulties and consider how this may fit into his or her IEP.
- To consider who should be a part of implementation and what information would shape this.

Insanity is doing the same thing over and over again and expecting different results. (Bill O'Hanlon)

If a child repeats the same behaviour over and over again, don't punish the child for repeating it, rather consider what is the underlying cause of the behaviour.

When you are riding a dead horse the best strategy is to dismount. (A Dakota tribal saying)

If you are in a hole, stop digging.

Negative behaviour

Why do children become frustrated and display negative behaviour, especially those with DCD?

Behaviour alters in all of us because of a number of influences – these can be broadly divided into:

Internal

- Conflict between what you are doing versus what you want to do.
- Demotivation – as a consequence of other difficulties.
- Oppositional defiant disorder or bipolar disorder – where there is probably a biochemical problem which causes mood disturbance.
- Lack of choice.
- Learning difficulty.

External

- Other children.
- Other adults.
- Environment.

The environment

The child with DCD is like any other child and will respond to situations in similar ways. Most children are born inquisitive about the world around them and will seek out information and answers. The three-year-old who says 'why?' after every adult answer becomes tiresome after a while, but is only seeking to understand the world around them. The busy toddler who touches everything in sight and wants to wander off around the next corner only wants to know what is there, and is not deliberately setting out to *try* to be naughty, but is explorative and inquisitive about the world around them.

Until recently, systems in education have put in place a behavioural modification approach to dealing with the child with negative behaviour patterns. The ecological approach is different, its key elements being changing teachers' negative perception of pupil behaviour to a positive interpretation, and teachers entering into a cooperative rather than confrontational relationship with the pupil. If the teacher no longer views certain behaviour as negative, then there is no longer a potentially oppositional nature to the situation. This requires counselling and psychotherapeutic skills that may need to be taught to the teacher (Molnar and Lindquist 1989).

Could we change the type of school for the child, rather than the child change for the school?

The Traditional School versus The Learning School

The Traditional School	The Learning School
Problem situation defined as being the student's problem	Problem situation defined as being a problem with the learning environment
Weak sense of community	Cooperative school
Authoritarian social control	Democratic social control
Student-diagnosing problem-solving (biomedical and psychological models)	Systems thinking in problem-solving (social model)
Beliefs reflect positivism	Beliefs reflect constructionism
Goal is to deal with school's targets	Official goal is to deal with each student's individuality
Set curriculum for all children to follow	Ability to adapt curriculum to meet the needs of the child

(Adapted from Naukkarinen 1999, pp. 243–4)

What happens to the child when starting school?

It is this inquisitiveness and free will to explore that is stifled at times, when the constraints of having many children in a classroom requiring 'control' start to become a conflict for both the child and the teacher. Thirty children wandering around a school finding out what they want in their own time becomes unfeasible. However for some children their preferred learning style means that touching and feeling and doing are the best ways to learn. Passive listening really does just go in one ear and out the other. Reflect how adults behave when listening to a lecture. Many of us will 'fiddle', suck our pens, doodle, and become fidgety after a period of time, and find it hard to concentrate.

The arrival at school for some children will be the first time they have to conform, and have less choice in the way they can seek out information. Other people will now decide the way information is delivered and how learning is undertaken. The school setting imposes a restraint on the child and inadvertently seeks to reduce inquisitiveness. It aims to move the child towards conforming to the norm – sitting in class for periods of time and following set pieces of work at a pace dictated by the teacher rather than the child, and in a style chosen by the teacher.

The intrinsic motivation and eagerness to learn for learning's sake may be swapped for learning because the child has to. The child has to 'get through' the work. This can leave the child working to a certain level and seeing that he or she no longer needs to seek out more information – enough has been done. The teacher may exchange the internal motivation and drive the young child once showed, for external motivation and control. The child learns to seek approbation and rewards for work completed. Success is rated by marks and examinations rather than an internal interest and motivation to want to know more for him or herself.

The young child needs no encouragement to go out in the garden to explore the mud and look at worms as a part of a science expedition. They do not need to be made to listen to a story told by his or her mother. The child wants to, and will ask for more, and more, and more. The child has no external measure on him or her at this stage.

Some children see themselves as being put through a test that they are clearly going to fail. This is something that we are prepared to do to children but would never do to ourselves. (Compare this to sitting a driving test – we would carry on taking lessons until we thought we were ready.)

The control that is exerted on the child comes from the teacher, and that comes from the school. In a school where teachers are under greater pressure to perform, this pressure is then often passed on to their pupils in exerting greater control and giving them fewer opportunities for autonomy and choice in how they learn. Lack of choice in all of us can make us feel stressed and increase anxiety.

What has this got to do with the child with DCD? For children without learning difficulties, school imposes constraints but they can respond and perform to a level that is acceptable to others. This may mean the child does not 'over-try' but does what he or she needs to do to get by and stay out of trouble. This may not make for dynamic and exciting learning but it keeps the class 'under control'. Children without learning difficulties are more flexible. They learn to adapt and bend to meet the situation and can adapt and modify their behaviour from one situation to another. The child with DCD lacks adaptability and flexibility.

Adaptability and flexibility

The child with DCD finds it harder all round – in class and in the playground and at home. They cannot mix as well, they do not have the same language to join in and participate in quick playground banter, their work seems to be untidy and they are perceived to make less effort. Their peers perceive them as not as bright, not as able, and not as quick. The child from the age of around six years recognises that they are different from their peers. It starts to be measured in a number of ways in school.

Recognising the cause not the effect

Last in the running race.

Late for PE.

Writing and drawing looks like the work of a younger child.

Finds it harder to make friends.

Not asked to parties by other children.

Pushes a child and gets pushed back.

Walking around on the edge of the playground.

The child with DCD does not always have the advantage of being able to use all learning styles effectively. As with most of us, one or two routes seem to be better than others. In general, they learn better through the visual and kinaesthetic route rather than the auditory route, as short-term auditory memory is often poor.

Many classes, especially at secondary school, will be more 'talk and chalk' as pupil numbers are larger and a curriculum has to be covered in the most efficient way. For the DCD child this may mean potentially huge gaps in their acquisition of new material, the ability to record it and organise work in a methodical way. This leaves the child with a feeling of both frustration and confusion, wanting to learn but not being given materials in a format that they can take in and absorb.

Interference with learning can lead to frustration and cause alteration in behaviour patterns		
Difficulty	**Behaviour**	**Consequence**
Poor auditory memory	Difficulty understanding a series of commands. Not able to record homework – so not able to complete homework.	Asking for the command to be repeated several times. Appears not to be listening. Told off for not completing homework – child becomes frustrated and irritable.
Difficulty with balancing/sitting on the floor	Moving around, getting up.	Seen as distracting others, and inattentive.

Difficulty	Behaviour	Consequence
Difficulty with abstract language	Difficulty in mathematics.	Opts out, inattentive.
Difficulty writing at speed	The child's hand aches from holding the pen too tight.	Writes short pieces, and gets told off for not making an effort.
Difficulty listening in a busy environment – auditory/perceptual difficulties	Seen to be looking around and not concentrating.	Thought not to be trying.
Poor fine motor coordination	Slow to change for PE – late to return to next lesson.	Told off for being late.
Difficulty with pragmatic language, e.g. teacher uses idioms and metaphors such as raining cats and dogs, pull up your socks	Child sees this literally and answers back that it is not true, or does not see it as a request and ignores it.	Child seen and told off as being insolent.
Poor organisational skills Writing task	Leaves books at home.	Told off.
	Avoidance strategies – will ask to go to the toilet, walks around the room, offers to help other children, makes a joke.	Seen as lazy, distractible, wilful.

Strategies for these difficulties are determined by the underlying reasons. These are discussed in the relevant chapters. Task analysis also will then determine how the teacher decides on the appropriate remediation.

Behaviour patterns

The child with DCD may end up displaying negative behaviour or disruptive behaviour, not because they are trying to gain attention but rather because their difficulties impose constraints on their ability to concentrate and carry out tasks, and this has a knock-on effect on behaviour. Having to concentrate, balance, listen, think and record can be just too much and creates overflow for the child, and this becomes symptomatic in words or actions.

It is as if the child only has so much room in his or her 'stress bucket' and if it becomes overfull then they show the signs and symptoms of stress and anxiety, which show themselves as negative behaviour. Consider how we behave as adults when we are stressed. We shout, reach for a drink, and become irritable with those around us. A stressed adult shows deterioration in their level of work and becomes irritable and agitated. These are very similar signs to those that we see in the DCD child under pressure.

Commonly the younger child with DCD will usually behave well at school and will display negative behaviour once he or she reaches home. This then moves to a change in style of behaviour as the child gets older, and if they are then not receiving adequate support or understanding they will typically start to 'act out' their frustrations at school as well as at home. They will usually do this in one of two ways, either by no longer bothering, opting out (developing 'sod it' syndrome), or displaying disruptive behaviour in and out of the classroom. This is quite hard to distinguish from normal teenage rebellious behaviour. However the child with DCD is often emotionally younger than his or her peers so will go through teenage rebellion at a later stage.

Understanding the reasons for negative or oppositional behaviour
Often the first assumption when we see a child repeating the same negative behaviour is that the child is being 'naughty', rather than considering that this is a way of telling us he or she is finding it harder to do something. Many children have tried to tell another that they have a problem, but if they have not been heard or understood then they give up and 'act out' their struggle.

The child with DCD may have language processing difficulties, which make it harder for them to clearly think through and vocalise where their difficulties lie and what their problems are. This may be why he or she is struggling and ending up acting out rather than saying what is wrong. He or she may also have attempted at one time to do so, and have been dismissed as 'not trying, not bothering, being lazy, etc.'. One attempt at trying to ask for help may have felt like one attempt too many.

Lauren, 7 years

Lauren had enjoyed her summer holiday and had been having children around to play for short times with some success. In the past she found undirected play difficult and she would tend to lead play and be a poor winner and loser. She was better when an adult was around to guide play and minimise disasters so that she had a good experience to model her behaviour on next time. Lauren has non-verbal learning difficulties as a part of her DCD, and is not always quick to adapt to change and interpret social nuances.

A new term at school and a new teacher have caused deterioration in her behaviour. Within two weeks of the start of term, Lauren is having sleep disturbance on all school nights, but not on Fridays and Saturdays.

What should this be telling us?

What parent/teacher liaison work needs to be done so that there is awareness by both parties of behaviour/difficulties in school and at home and how one impacts on another?

What you see is not always what you get!

Child writes only one sentence during the lesson and answers the wrong question.

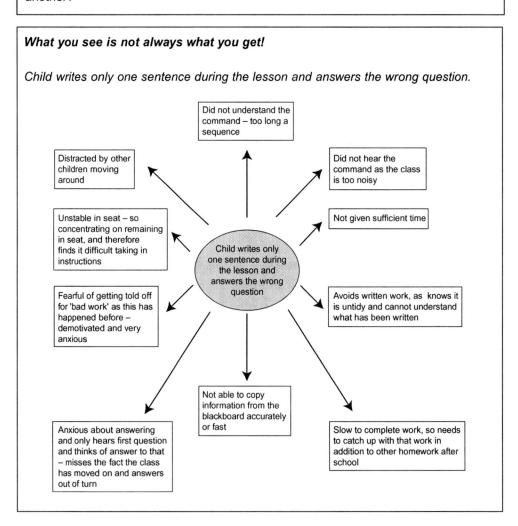

Jo, 6 years

The teacher told me that Jo loved writing on the keyboard in class: in fact every time he had the opportunity he would spend as long as possible and wrote some exciting and interesting stories. In a class of 30, unfortunately Jo was only allowed to have access to the class computer occasionally. The teacher said that he had a real problem with Jo, because *every* time Jo had to do some free writing he would crawl under the table and the only person able to get him out was the head teacher, who would take Jo into her room and let him do some work on her computer until the end of class. Jo's teacher found this all very disturbing and it could take up half the class time as Jo crawled from under one table to another, being chased around the room. The teacher also reported that Jo has very poor handwriting and is frustrated by it.

Why do children behave like Jo? – The greatest clue to all of this is '*every*'. If every time one thing happens another action happens we need to consider *why*. One way to stop this behaviour could be to punish Jo and stop him going on the computer until he stops crawling under the table. Is this the right approach? Another is to consider why this behaviour started in the first place and to look how to support Jo so that he no longer needs to display it. Which one would you choose?

We could offer to give Jo a reward for the type of behaviour we want to see, but does this solve the problem? Yes, it may do in the short term, but it does not solve anything in the long term and is ending up controlling the situation, i.e. making sure that Jo does not disturb the rest of the class, but has no effect in supporting Jo through his own problem.

Why do some children seem to learn the school rules faster than others? – Often in school we expect children to conform to class norms, when sometimes they have not had examples of these shown to them by parents before entering school, or have not attended nursery to have behaviour modelled. The impact of this on most children is fairly small and we know that by half term most children in infant school will have settled down and understood the rules of the school and start to conform to them, even if they have not had previous experience of these at home.

Robert, 5 years

Robert came to school every morning very hungry and usually late. Home was pretty chaotic and Robert has come to school at times with trousers but no underwear. He usually has not had breakfast. When Robert arrived at school he had never sat at a table to eat a meal, or used a knife and fork. Most suppers consisted of noodles in a pot in front of the television or a packet of chips eaten with his fingers.

The school ensured that Robert went to a breakfast club and that he also had school lunches. The other children learnt quite quickly to eat lunch neatly, but Robert was seen to be extremely messy and found cutting and spreading tasks impossible. He would end up using his fingers and be told off by the teacher and lunch supervisors for being messy.

Robert also showed other signs of poor fine motor coordination, such as being slow to change for PE and needing help with buttons and shoes. His colouring and cutting also still seemed very immature.

Modelling good behaviour is not always enough for the child with DCD – Early experiences at meal times for many children allow them to learn social skills as well as skills such as using cutlery which are a precursor for handwriting – undertaking a two-handed activity cooperatively. Lack of skill because of lack of exposure early on for some children is not such a problem unless their underlying foundation skills are poor.

For the child with DCD this has a double effect. Missing out at an early age on being able to practise these skills impacts on social development – learning how to converse, take turns, attend and stay at the table for a period of time, and also to practise using two hands in a cooperative manner. The child may already have poor basic building blocks, and be starting out at 'level 2' when he or she arrives at school without any foundations or 'level 1' in place. This is why there is often a time-lag in acquisition that is far greater than expected because the child has to learn a complete set of skills as well as continuing to learn what is presented to him or her on a daily basis.

This is where the social difficulties and coordination difficulties of DCD are closely allied. If you do not have the good non-verbal skills to pick up how others are seeing you, you may not have the inner motivation to see that it is necessary to change.

Even in very early years the normal acquisition of non-verbal skills may be seen to be delayed. The young child may not be able to interpret the facial gestures of others and distinguish between a happy grin and a grimace, even from his or her mother. This may be due to a neurological reason, i.e. poor transfer of information from one area of the brain, or may be due to lower tone leading to poorer eye-to-eye contact. This is discussed more fully Chapter 8.

Rules and consequences

Rules – implicit or explicit?
When children arrive at school they need to understand a host of rules. When to stand up or sit down, when to say 'Miss' or 'Sir' and how to relate to their peers are just a few of them. There may be class rules and school rules. Some of these will be clearly spelt out and may even be displayed on the walls of the class. These are the explicit rules that are usually easy to learn because they are emphasised and repeated.

There are also a host of implied rules that most children pick up by watching other people and listening to them because they want to fit in with their peer group. Implied rules may vary from one setting to another and also the child needs to be able to understand that behaviour in one setting may be inappropriate in another. The child may need to learn that to succeed means doing what the teacher says and living up to the teacher's expectations of proper behaviour (whatever this means: and it may vary from one teacher to another, and in the same teacher at different times).

The child with DCD may have problems with both implicit rules and explicit ones for differing reasons. The explicit rules are usually clearer to see than the implicit ones, especially if they are both spoken and recorded for future reference. The DCD child often lacks flexibility and adaptability to different situations, and may not be able to see that a rule in one situation may not be appropriate in another, e.g. sitting quietly in class may be appropriate in one lesson such as Circle Time when the teacher may be telling a story, but may be inappropriate and unnecessary in singing lessons or in PE.

Sam, 9 years

His teacher told Sam that a piece of work he completed was excellent when he got 8/10 for it. 'That was the best piece of work, you should try to achieve this again,' his teacher said. Sam tried desperately to achieve this mark again all term, and became upset one day. The teacher could not understand it as Sam had got 10/10 for a test that morning. He asked him why he was upset. Sam replied, ' I didn't get 8/10: you told me that that was excellent and that was what I should achieve again.' You can see that a seemingly harmless comment can be misconstrued.

Implicit rules may be much harder for the child with DCD as he or she needs good observation skills to pick up social nuances and also needs to be able to transfer a rule and adapt it to another setting.

Andrew, 6 years

Andrew was in school and was seen crying in the playground one lunchtime. The teacher went up to him and asked him what was wrong. Andrew said the other children were laughing at him when he went to the toilet. He said he didn't know what he was doing that was so funny. The next day the teacher followed Andrew into the toilet without Andrew knowing that he was there. Andrew stood in front of the urinals and proceeded to drop his trousers completely – bottom displayed for all to see as they came in. All was revealed in more ways than one!

The teacher had a word with Andrew's mum that afternoon at the end of the day. Andrew had problems being able to stand at the urinal in a stable position, and be able to point appropriately and not wet his trousers because of his poor coordination. The only way that he could manage was to pull his trousers right down. At home this was not a problem but Andrew was not even slightly aware of the impact of being fully undressed in this way in front of his peers, and how he would be ridiculed for it. He was not able to see that a behaviour in one setting may not be acceptable at all in another setting.

Discussion – Can you think of other examples where a child may have difficulties adapting to differing situations? What implicit rules do you have in your school?

How do the physical aspects of DCD impact on behaviour?

From an early age the child may not have been able to have good eye-to-eye contact with others, so has not had practice in understanding the difference between varied facial expressions. Other children would have had the practice in picking up facial gestures and cues, and by school age would not only be able to recognise angry, sad, happy and frightened, but a host of other emotions such as irritable, anxious and excited. This means that the child with DCD may well be less able at non-verbal learning skills. This is discussed in more depth in Chapter 8.

Muscle tone also has an effect on posture and poor postural tone impacts in a number of ways. Others may misjudge the child and see them as being slovenly or lazy as they 'flop' on to the chair or lay across their desk. They may actually require special support such as seating wedges and angle boards to enable them to do a task such as reading or writing while maintaining their sitting posture on the chair.

Poor tone may be misinterpreted in important situations such as an interview. When meeting others for the first time, low tone and anxiety may mean that the individual with DCD may have a 'sloppy' handshake, poor eye contact and may sit down in a slouched sitting position. As a consequence, the individual may well be rejected for something that he or she is completely unaware of. Their potential skills for the job may be forgotten and first impressions may end up being the last ones as well.

Difficulties in school and home behaviour

Difficulties in school can have consequences on behaviour at home. Regular negative behaviour at home may make parents consider that their style of parenting is poor, and the consequences of this may be to increase discipline at home and restrict and punish the child for his or her behaviour.

The parent may ask the teacher how their child behaves when in school only to be told that they behave very well. This only leads to reinforce the parents' conviction that it is something that 'they' are doing.

Could there be another explanation?

The child may be feeling out of his or her depth in school and be struggling with some of the tasks being given to them. Most children with DCD are not in the category of school-refuser and want to go to school despite their difficulties. They want to please their teacher at this stage and are internally motivated to do well. They also want to make friends and be accepted by their peer group.

Pop-crackle-snap!

Displays of negative behaviour can often develop into a 'flip-out' or rage attack that can last minutes or even longer. For the parent this can be what they see at the end of every day.

Rage attacks

Some children with DCD have more than the odd temper tantrum: they have rage attacks. These can last from minutes to hours and can seem to happen with little warning: although if closely observed, the child may show signs and symptoms such as their ears going red, or they may start to move in an agitated way and start mumbling.

The child seems to have no control once the attack has started; it is as if the champagne cork has popped and the only option is to allow all of the champagne to be emptied out before the child can calm down. For some children the bottle seems very full and a very long time is needed to calm down.

These same children who exhibit this extreme behaviour often show signs of oppositional defiant disorder, and this is discussed in a book called *The Explosive Child* by Ross Greene (published by HarperCollins) which considers the diagnosis of bi-polar disease.

There are some children with DCD who have a clear overlap with these other conditions and will exhibit this behaviour typically. Sleep disturbance and faddy eating (craving sugar and salt) may also be seen typically in this group of children.

Temper tantrums

Why does the child with DCD have temper tantrums?

The child will typically display this behaviour at the end of the day at home. Is the behaviour a consequence of the day, rather than the effect of something Mum has done 'to' the child? This type of behaviour usually escalates if there has been a problem at school.

The child may see home as a safe haven and the

tension that has been bubbling up all day finally can no longer be controlled. The champagne bottle pops and explodes all over the person nearest to them, and this is usually the parent. This negative behaviour at home can be very wearing and has an impact on the whole family as well as the parent and child. Mum has to now spend time calming the child down at a time in the day where other siblings may also want and need attention. This can also put a strain on sibling relationships as well.

What strategies could help?

- Improved teacher/parent partnership working.
- Time out after the day – a walk with the dog, a swim.
- Protected time with a parent to talk through the day.
- Stay in school an extra five minutes and leave when it is a little quieter – or Mum come in to pick the child up if younger.

How could these problems be identified?

- How does behaviour vary between school and home?
- What liaison could and should take place between home and school?
- How, as a teacher, will you identify that this is happening, when the child may have only been in school for a short time and may not yet be identified as having a learning difficulty?
- Could you develop a checklist for home to highlight any areas of difficulty or concern that could provide a framework for discussion at parents' evenings or specific meetings?
- Could a parent keep a log and inform you if the behaviour gets worse or better?
- Could you ask the child to complete a visual rating scale, e.g. smiley face to sad face.

What happens to the adolescent child?

The older child may develop a 'sod it' syndrome mentality. That is, that if they remain misunderstood and their needs are not met, they will start acting out their frustrations in school as well as out, or just decide not to bother at all. This may be difficult to distinguish from normal teenage development where negative views of school and rules are often seen as the adolescent starting to develop an understanding of their own personal autonomy. This is the stage we all recognise if we have had a child going through puberty in our households, where any view a parent has on anything from food and holidays to music and politics will be diametrically opposed by the teenager.

Should we be trying to modify this type of negative behaviour? – Consider any children with specific learning difficulties and whether they are displaying opt-out or negative behaviour – are there any classes where they are doing well and that they seem to enjoy, compared to other classes? Why is this? Ask the child what he or she likes and hates. You may be surprised that this will reveal a great deal.

We all want success…

- A quick fix – We often seek something that is going to solve *our* problems rather than consider the underlying causes.

Tim, 16 years

Tim wants to be a computer programmer when he leaves school and is certainly very talented in this area. He has designed the school website and has networked the school computer system. Yet Tim cannot write legibly and is aware of this, as of course are his teachers. He hates English lessons because of the recording that is required. He has been given extra lessons in English to practise his handwriting.

He has ended up in detention on a number of occasions as he 'forgets' to do the homework. He is then punished and no longer allowed to go to the computer club, the one thing in school that he enjoys! He has now decided not to bother with the school website and will not maintain it.

How else could this have been managed?

What is the underlying problem?

What motivates Tim – could this not be used as an area to help with his English?

Is the punishment appropriate or justified?

What help, rather than punishment, could have been put into place?

- Sometimes we want magic cures – We all want these at times even though we know they are very rare events!
- Little investment in time or effort – It may be hard to see that time invested now in sorting out the underlying problem may be time well spent, when there are 30 children in the class and one is being disruptive and you need to get through the curriculum.
- Why should I be the one to change? – There is sometimes reluctance on the part of others to change something in them to meet the needs of the child, rather than the child always being the one that is seen as 'wrong'. There are no wrongs and rights and many children have to fit into round holes when they are square pegs. Teaching today is perhaps more prescriptive, and this makes it harder to adapt the classroom to different pupils who may require different ways of being taught.
- Use what has worked before in other situations – Sometimes it is hard to see why strategies that seem to have been successful before are not having the same level of success with the child with DCD.

'Listen to me, can't you hear what I am saying…?'

BUT are YOU listening?

Joseph, 7 years

In the literacy hour, all the children were expected to sit in a circle for some of the time each day to listen to a story. Joseph would end up being told off nearly every day for being fidgety and he would quite often end up wandering around the classroom. The teacher was finding it hard to think of ways to maintain Joseph's interest in the story, even though at other times he worked hard.

One thing she noticed was that if Joseph was sitting near to the walls of the class then he would always lean against them. An occupational therapist came into class one day to visit another child in the middle of story time just when Joseph was getting told off for getting up. The occupational therapist observed the situation and then quietly suggested that Joseph be allowed to sit on a low chair during story time. Joseph was having problems keeping still because his posture made it hard for him to maintain a sitting position without help, and he needed to be placed in a chair. After that day Joseph was quiet and attentive and joined in more when they discussed the stories. He was now supported, but also he was now better able to attend rather than using up most of his concentration on trying to remain stable.

Joseph had been misunderstood, and was thought to be being naughty and also inattentive and distractible. He could have been labelled inappropriately as having Attention Deficit and Hyperactivity Disorder.

Approaches that will not help the child

If change is to be seen, then there needs to be an understanding why strategies that have been tried before have failed. There needs to be:

- buy-in by you as teacher/parent;
- buy-in by the child to need to/want to/or be able to change.
- The child may already be seen as 'disabled', or as having a behaviour problem.
- The solutions being tried may start at where the child is already having problems, and not work out from where there are successes in the child's life.
- A label or diagnosis may have been given to the child, which now seems permanently tattooed on: rather than being 'temporarily stuck on' and the child regarded as having a 'behaviour problem'. The problem with this is that doing something about a problem usually means doing something *to* the child, rather than the child being involved in the problem.
- Perceptions by others may be preconceived and based on previous experience. You sometimes hear people saying 'I had a boy with DCD, he always did…', implying that all children with DCD are the same. Or 'I tried that with the child in my class and it didn't work', implying that the same techniques are successful or fail on all children: an oversimplified assumption.
- A trial of one sort of help may leave us feeling that everything else we may try could be more of the same.

- What happens to some people who had difficulties throughout their lives? Not everyone who had behaviour problems or difficulties at school ended up a waster or a loser. For example, Einstein, dyslexic, physicist; David Bailey, dyspraxic, photographer; Steve Redgrave, dyslexic.

The moral is maybe that you can succeed in life despite not being able to kick a ball or colour-in, and that problems that seem huge in school are often irrelevant later on in life. Not being able to play in a team is not a prerequisite for life: not being able to use a pair of scissors is not the end of the world, although we may have struggled over these things at school. It may be that the struggles that make some children with DCD more resilient and able to understand strife in others, lead them to careers in the caring professions or as journalists or photographers, they being able to have an understanding of other people's feelings.

If we are to consider the child's viewpoint and difficulties then we need to see that the child *has* a problem rather than *is* the problem.

Discussion
- Take a minute or two to think and then write down what are the long-term goals you would like for all children in school, not just those with DCD.
- What would you like them to be able to do – what is important as opposed to what is necessary?
- What are the criteria for success in adult life?
- What parts of your life have contributed to your success and failure?
- What did you learn in school and from whom, that you remember now and had an effect on you?

Compare the following two sets of survival skills to get you through your school days and your adult life.

Children's survival skills
- To conform in school setting.
- Compliance.
- To pass tests set by others well enough to get on to the next stage in life.
- Not to criticise others in any position of power, e.g. teacher.
- To take punishment if given – even if the child does not understand why he or she is being punished.
- Not to try too hard otherwise more will be expected of the child next time – giving back what is expected.
- To perform rather than learn.

Tests are sometimes used to identify the failing school but sometimes miss out identifying the failing child.

Adult survival skills
- Independent living skills – to be able to organise and look after ourselves.
- Socially able and confident.
- Consider and make decisions.
- Think critically and be creative.
- Good self-esteem.

Consider a strategy for success – rewards and punishments
Praise is a powerful tool.

Not handled properly, it can be a negative force, a kind of drug that, rather than strengthening students, makes them passive and dependent on the opinion of others.

(Carol Dweck from *Self Theories: their role in motivation* (Dweck 1999))

Rewards and punishments are similar although often seen as opposites. The child who fails to get a reward has been punished. The child who avoids punishment has been rewarded.

The two ways of gaining a successful learning outcome do not usually work for a number of reasons.

There has been research to show that rewards and punishments are usually set by others (usually the teacher) and immediately have a controlling effect on the child. The end-point, whether negative or positive, has usually been predetermined and the child has not been given a choice in the outcome. This immediately sets up a ' them versus us' mentality and the child may become over-reliant on the basis of the reward. The child may think it is not worth doing any extra work beyond that which gives him or her the reward, as there is no point. Extra effort does not always mean extra reward and this may be a reward that after a time becomes less meaningful.

The reward may be set for example to encourage a child to read more books. The child could be given a prize for every book they read. The clever child will learn quickly to read only short books so that he or she can get through more. Sadly the aim of opening up the child's mind to want to read and gain pleasure is often diminished from this experience. There is even evidence to show that this ends up in the child wanting to do less of the activity after the reward has been removed. Has the child taken in the information in the book, thought about it and considered its meaning, or just got through it as quickly as possible? Probably the latter. Reading schemes where there is a competitive element within a class can sometimes lead to children reading a lot but comprehending very little.

The child becomes less motivated by his or her own own internal drive to learn and enjoy the book, and more by a desire to please others, leading to being externally controlled and motivated. This does not lead the child to gain the skills we want in adulthood. It does allow a class to conform: a short-term choice that is often made to get through a pressured curriculum.

How does this affect the child with DCD?

> The reward system sets up competition amongst a class rather than encouraging them to work together as a team to reach a goal. It implies that there will be losers and winners. The child with DCD may not be able to write as fast, or read as fast, and may be disadvantaged at the first hurdle. He may see little hope of ever being the first to finish anything and will eventually feel there is no point in even trying in the first place. Even IEPs where individual goals are set must be achievable for the child. The child should also know why he is learning a task, as it may seem pointless to him. He may need to see that there need to be seven tasks learnt before he can do the big one. Giving him a vision of what he is working towards is very important for the child with DCD, or he will feel he is always working on a repetitive task with no clear outcome. (Mueller and Dweck 1998)

Motivational techniques may also not work for similar reasons. For example, if you promised a child with DCD a trip to Disney World if he got in the rugby team, you would wait forever, as the child would know that however much he tried he would never succeed. It is the equivalent of asking a blind person to see. Phrases such as 'if you only tried harder you could do it' are fruitless to a child who is already working to full capacity, and serve only to demoralise the child further and not encourage him or her more.

Praise can sometimes not be the solution either. The child may wait for praise after a task and learn to become over-reliant on external views of his or her ability rather than seeing their own successes for themselves. We have all seen adults who seek out praise and only seem happy if they are constantly told how good they are. It may also make the individual worried and feel pressurised to perform well for others. It also can produce a lower interest in the task itself. Praise for praise itself is no good if the individual does not know why he or she is being praised and what for. It is also ineffective if given too often and to some children and not others.

Creating a template for success

1. Consider how you can create the best environment for the child to succeed, not fail

If we want a flower to grow we make sure that the environment and conditions are right. We make sure there is sufficient food, water and light. For the child with DCD and similar difficulties, we need to make sure conditions are right to make it most conducive for the child to learn. We are more used to assessing needs for the physically disabled. If there was a child in class in a wheelchair, then we would make sure there were ramps or lifts to enable the child to get from A to B. The same approach is true for the DCD child. Ensuring an appropriate environment will increase the chances of success rather than failure. We would not tell a child who was visually impaired to read, and feel disappointed when he or she failed to do so. We would not tell that child that they only need to try harder and they would succeed. We would ensure that there were appropriate tools for the child to do the job, such as Braille books. The same is true for the DCD child, e.g. where handwriting is a difficulty. We sometimes tell the child to 'try harder' or 'write it out again' when clearly this will not help a great deal and will further demoralise the child and reduce their desire to be creative.

2. Keep a log
- Where and when are there difficulties or tantrums in school?
- How often does it happen?
- What does the child look like when having a tantrum – what is the verbal and non-verbal behaviour?
- What does he or she say/feel?
- How long does the behaviour last?
- What do *you* say and do during the behaviour?
- What do you do and say afterwards?

You need this information before you can make a judgement on a child's behaviour, so that you can understand the behaviour prior to the negative behaviour, and how you and others around you reacted before and after. This is especially true when behaviour is recurring. You are looking for patterns to see what triggers the reaction.

3. Discussion about change
Consider how you can ensure that the child has some choice in what they are doing and allow sufficient time for the child to prepare and adapt to change. The DCD child is slower and less flexible than other children. An exciting day out planned at the last moment can be great for the rest of the class, but for the child with DCD

Behaviour Log		
Name:		
Date:		Additional notes
Where and when did the behaviour occur?		
How long did it last?		
What does he/she look like before?		
What does he/she look like during?		
What does he/she look like after?		
With whom was interaction taking place?		
What did the observer see during?		
What did the observer see after?		
What happened to resolve it?		
Did the child show remorse?		

> **So you see a pattern – what can be changed?**
> - Change the pattern.
> - Change your response.
> - Change the place.
> - Create the tantrum – get the child to 'recreate it'.
> - Do you have a fixed belief that you need to alter?
> - Do you resist the change rather than the child?

can be a nightmare of changes and confusion leading to a high anxiety state. The child may not know where they are going, what will happen when they get there and when they will return. All this will cause the child to react in a negative way. The lack of flexibility will only lead to one option, and that is to snap rather than bend.

4. Provide ideas how to improve
Provide ideas rather than just say it is wrong or you do not like it – a child needs a framework to improve. Being given this is not cheating but being shown.

5. Consider what you are testing
Make sure the ground rules are fair, e.g. writing – perhaps this could be just shapes and forms. A spelling test – does this need to be timed, and could it be given via a tape so that the child can listen to the same word several times? Could someone else record the response for the child?

6. Decide what is important
Consider working on only what is important rather than on everything.

7. Make learning interesting and active
Classes should be noisy and quiet – 'keeping the class under control' usually means a quiet class – does it mean a learning class? The DCD child usually learns better by seeing and doing and verbalising to reinforce the learning. Listening alone is very hard to do. What do we do when we are in a lecture? Some of us doodle; others chew the end of the pen. We are still listening, but we need to do these things to reinforce our learning and thinking. All children need to have some flexibility in the way they learn.

8. Use logical persuasion
- How could you reframe your request?

- Are you interested in changing the way you present it into a language that encourages success, not discourages it?
- How could the child be given choices and not just a brick wall?

9. Explain rules and consequences
- Let the child choose the consequence.
- What is time out and where is time out – does the child understand these concepts and see the reason for them, or are they given to him or her in the middle of a 'strop'?

10. KISS (Keep it simple stupid!)
- The simple telling-off – consider in current practice where you may give a longer version when a more simple one would do.

If one word will do, then use it, rather than giving a long explanation for the behaviour and why you do not like it and why you would prefer it was changed and how he or she is different from other children and...

11. Understand how YOU react to stress
- What do you do if you have had a bad day?
- Why should children be any different?
- Do you have a mixed ethos – you can shout/kick the cat, but children cannot!

In the end we need to understand why children behave the way they do, and if what we see is in response to the way we are 'working' with the child, and what we want to produce as an end product. The DCD child finds it hard to fit a set mode and needs to be understood and appropriately supported to meet his or her needs, otherwise the behaviour we see is to be expected.

Factory produced children – conform to a set specification, pass the tests, uniform, fail if below a certain level of quality, narrow focus of skills, pass the tests but lack life skills
  or
Free range organically produced children – individual, creative, able to integrate, work as a part of a team, risk-take, pride and ownership of task, free-thinking, ambitious, continuing to learn, problem-solving

---

References

Molnar, A. and Lindquist, B. (1989) *Changing Problem Behavior in Schools.* San Francisco: Jossey-Bass.

Mueller, C.M. and Dweck, C.S. (1998) 'Intelligence praise can undermine motivation and performance', *Journal of Personality and Social Psychology*, 75, 33–52.

Naukkarinen, A. (1999) 'Balancing rigor and relevance. Developing problem-solving associated with students' challenging behavior in the light of a study of an upper comprehensive school'. *Jyvaskyla Studies in Education, Psychology and Social Research* 149, University of Jyvaskyla.

CHAPTER 10

Intervention – research and treatments

Learning objectives
- To critically analyse why and how we intervene with children and adults with DCD.

Learning outcomes
- To gain an understanding of the intervention processes.
- To gain an understanding of research methodologies, and how to critically review new or current treatments for effectiveness.

Introduction

The ever-increasing demands on available resources in meeting the needs of individuals with DCD suggests that services in the future will need to consider intervention in new and innovative ways, and not perhaps relying on what has been done in the past. For parents, the perception is often that there is a key to unlock all; for the teacher or therapist under pressure there is a need to have something easy to deliver. However, many of the children, as discussed in previous chapters, have overlapping difficulties, making the ready-made instant treatment unlikely to exist, as each child requires a tailored package to meet their needs. There is a need to consider the child's cultural and social background as well as previous experiences that will colour his or her approach to education and therapy. This may have additional overlays where the parents may have specific learning difficulties as well, and may have had negative experiences that are recalled as they see their child having similar difficulties.

Remediation approaches for individuals with DCD

Intervention techniques for children with DCD are varied and the efficacy of these interventions is controversial. Historically, approaches to intervention have focused on remediating the underlying processing deficits, based on the assumption that there is a direct relationship between underlying processes and functional performance. Research also suggests that given the heterogeneity of DCD, no single approach works for all children.

Activity/task analysis

Children with DCD learn from an early age that they find it harder to do many things. They also do not like to be identified as being different from their peer group. Therefore it is important that intervention implemented is contextual, inclusive and integrated into everyday learning and living situations.

In order to ensure that the individual is able to learn a task 'activity', it is important that it meets the needs of the individual. 'Activities' used are therefore born out of good assessment.

The process of breaking down an activity into stages can be summarised as 'activity analysis'. Each stage is analysed for relevance to remediation requirements, which comprise the following characteristics: to determine the potential of an activity for grading, i.e. to make it harder or easier to meet the needs of the child; and adaptation, i.e. to enable the child to access the activity.

The characteristics
Physical
- Physical abilities for competent performance
  - gross motor coordination
  - fine motor coordination
  - eye/hand coordination
  - dexterity
  - endurance

Sensory
- Touch: discrimination, protection, proprioception, kinaesthesia
- Visual: perception – colour, size, shape, constancy, figureground, acuity, ocular motor
- Auditory: perception, acuity
- Gustatory: taste
- Olfactory: smell
- Vestibular: movement

Psychological
- Insight
- Self-esteem
- Confidence
- Motivation

Organisation
- Structured: rules, manageable steps, pre-organised/pre-planned
- Unstructured: no specific steps/free-flowing

Social
- Verbal
- Non-verbal
- Group, individual, pairs
- Safety

Cognitive
- Level of thinking and functioning in relation to objects and activity – does the task require:
  - long-/short-term memory
  - attention/concentration
  - orientation to time, place, person (temporal)
  - directions for performance – writing, verbal, reading
  - abstract thinking
  - problem solving
  - symbolic interpretation
  - the use of already known information, or provide opportunities to learn experience by trial or error

Continuity
- All the activities must have a beginning and an end
- Activities should have a mechanism for justifying performance and *monitoring progress*. Starting and ending a task gives a sense of *achievement*

Task/environmental adaptation

Having analysed the component parts of the activity and its prospects for grading, it is essential that the 'teacher' is able to apply the activity to the requirements of the individual. In order to do this it may be necessary to adapt the activity or equipment from the usual method of performance to achieve optimum potential.

Adaptations should, where possible, be discussed with both the individual and the family in order to maintain cooperation. Adaptations should not bewilder nor alarm the individual to the extent he or she can no longer concentrate on the activity.

Adaptation of activity to compensate for difficulties
- Alteration to the equipment.
- Eliminate a stage of the activity.
- Change the individual's method of doing the activity.
- Change the environment.

General points to consider when choosing an activity
- Account to be taken of the individual's physical and cognitive level of function.
- Psychological state – motivation, perception and attitudes.
- Where the work is to be carried out.
- Time and resources available.
- Opportunities for differentiation and extension.
- Adult role/support required.

Problems with this approach
- Lack of resources.
- Timetable does not support the teaching staff.
- The school does not support differing teaching styles.

Discussion – Consider how you would grade a task to teach component skills if necessary. In some instances you may need to splinter skills teach, adapt the environment or the activity/tool – state how you would do this. Also consider the teaching method, i.e. demonstration, modelling, behavioural approach, etc.

Bottom-up approaches to intervention

- Sensory integration – The concept of sensory integration comes from a body of work developed by Jean Ayres PhD, OTR. As an Occupational Therapist, Dr Ayres was interested in the way in which sensory processing and motor planning disorders interfered with daily life, function and learning. The approach was originally developed for children with learning disabilities. It was designed to provide the child with the appropriate sensory stimulation to promote motor adaptation and learning.
- Process-orientated treatment – This approach was proposed by Laslo and

Bairstow, and is based on the premise that kinaesthesia (movement sense) is integral to the acquisition and performance of skilled motor behaviour.
- Perceptual motor training – This approach assumes a causal relationship between motor behaviour and underlying perceptual processes. Training involves providing the child with a broad range of experiences with sensory and motor tasks.

Top-down approaches

Recent thinking in movement science has emphasised a problem-solving approach to motor skill acquisition. Gentile (1992) noted that to approach treatment, the therapist must become an active problem-solver utilising a broad knowledge base to generate ways of helping the particular individual who is attempting to achieve a specific functional goal. Approaches based on a problem-solving premise are only now just beginning to emerge, and much literature is still theoretical. Recent examples of top-down approaches include (i) task specific intervention and (ii) cognitive approaches.
- Task specific – This approach focuses on direct teaching of the task to be learned. It is based on the premise that performance is the result of learning. Teaching the task is accomplished in steps, breaking the task down into smaller units, teaching each unit separately and then linking up all the units.
- Cognitive approaches – There are three approaches to be considered which all use problem-solving as the basis for remediation:
  Five inter-related steps to guide motor skill acquisition (Bouffard and Wall 1990)
    1. *Problem identification* – the child identifies the nature of the problem to be solved
    2. *Problem representation* – the child generates an appropriate, accurate depiction of the motor problem
    3. *Plan construction* – the child forms a plan to solve the problem and explore alternatives
    4. *Plan execution*
    5. *Evaluation of progress*
  Cognitive Motor Approach (Henderson and Sugden 1992). Based on an information-processing framework, consisting of a three-step process
    1. *Movement planning* – the child evaluates whether the task is attainable
    2. *Movement execution* – the child uses the plan to guide execution
    3. *Movement evaluation* – the child monitors progress
  The Cognitive Orientation to daily Occupational Performance (CO-OP) (Polatajko *et al.* 2001). This approach has roots in problem-solving through

verbal self-instruction. Generalisations and transfer of skills are promoted through the ecological relevance of tasks being addressed.

Although top-down approaches are congruent with contemporary motor learning theories, the evidence regarding the potential to improve motor skills and functional performance of children with DCD is only beginning to accumulate (Mandich *et al.* 2001).

Effectiveness of intervention

Mandich *et al.* 2001, in their review of treatments that have contemporary approaches drawn from human movement science, propose that treatment methods be based on the assumption that skill acquisition emerges from the interaction of the child, the task and the environment. They highlight the fact that little evidence exists to suggest any one approach is better than another. Given current demands for evidence-based practice, and evolving concepts in skill acquisition, a movement toward interventions that are based on functional outcomes is recommended. Certainly Polatajko *et al.* in their work using a cognitive approach have seen success in motor skills as well as self-esteem.

Sugden and Chambers' recent study (1998) also demonstrates that the types of treatments that have been used in the past either concentrate on the underlying motor skills and purport to improve areas such as kinaesthesia or sensory motor processes, or they tend to concentrate on teaching functional tasks aiming to specifically intervene in the deficient areas. Evaluations of these approaches show that they both work, producing significant improvements over control groups, but show no differences between either type of approach. It is hypothesised by Sugden and Chambers that there are more general principles involved in producing the effect, such as accurate assessment and tailoring activities to meet the needs of the individual child. Further, it is suggested that work with non-specialists in the motor area, such as teachers and parents, is a way forward with all but the most severely affected children.

Alternative therapies

As a teacher/health professional you may be asked your opinion on a new or existing treatment. In the last few years a few new 'therapies' have sprung up and have been claimed to be 'cures' for DCD. It is unlikely that there will be a single cure for a co-morbid condition so healthy scepticism should prevail.

It is therefore important to analyse and critically reflect upon the claims made. Some questions to consider are:

- *What is* the treatment?
- *What are* the claims?
- *Who is* making them?
- *Professional body* – what professional organisation does the person who is administering the 'treatment' belong to? What is their code of practice?
- *What training* have they undertaken?
- *Risk* – is there any risk to the individual in taking part?
- *Indemnity* – what has the company or individual in place in case of harm?
- *How is* the treatment supposed to work?
- *What evidence* is there for success? Is this anecdotal in nature?
- *Who can* be helped?
- *Who cannot* be helped?
- *How long* do you have to have the treatment for?
- *Are there* any side effects?
- *What evidence* is there to show the effects?
- *If studies* have been done – what size, how constructed, what are the long-term benefits, is there carry over, and how long does the individual have to continue treatment for?
- *What is* the cost of the treatment?

A way forward – the need for collaboration and partnership working

The desirability of a collaborative approach has been recommended in many health and education reports and in subsequent legislation. A wide range of professionals is likely to be involved in the care of an individual with DCD. However difficulties often arise when attempting to work in collaboration because the professionals are usually employed by different public services and consequently have differing priorities. This can lead to more conflict than cooperation. Clearly government initiatives are recognising the value and importance of joint working between Health and Education to provide a seamless service. The new Code of Practice makes clear the importance of external agencies in helping schools identify, assess and make provision for individuals with special educational needs.

In order to achieve partnership working it is vital to have structures in place to enable collaboration, in other words staff agree to pursue the same goals in a coordinated manner. The implication is that a team of people can achieve more together than each could as individuals. The term 'synergy' has been used to summarise this process. However, Education has a long history of working alone with teachers being trained to be self-sufficient. Therefore the shift from working with pupils to working with other adults demands new skills. Hanko (1990) writes of the importance of joint problem-solving in order to greatly improve the solutions offered and to embed the services provided by Health within the school curriculum. In many ways Health and Education share cultures as both are concerned with progress and development, use assessment and devise programmes to meet individual needs.

Concept based theories such as multidisciplinary, interdisciplinary and transdisciplinary have all been used to describe the manner in which two or more professions from different disciplines work together. Orelove & Sobsey (1991) suggest the term 'multidisciplinary' as professionals from more than one discipline working alongside but separately from each other. The term 'interdisciplinary' is where professionals share information and decide on education programmes together. These programmes are implemented separately by members of the individual disci-

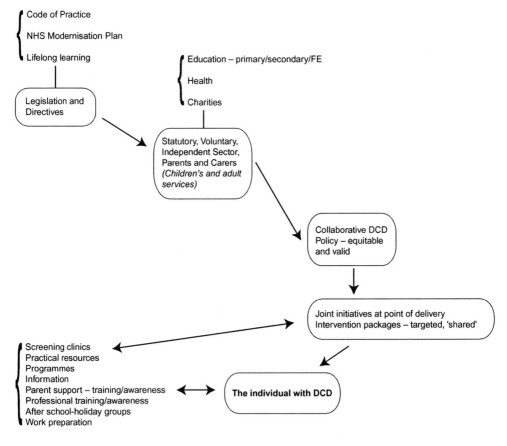

Figure 10.1   A framework for collaborative service delivery

plines. Finally Orelove and Sobsey describe the term 'transdisciplinary', which they feel is the most developed model of working with children with special needs. This involves sharing or transferring information and skills across traditional disciplinary boundaries to enable one or two team members to be the primary workers supported by others working as consultants. It is the final model of 'transdisciplinary' working which this partnership has been based upon. Here therapists act as consultants to teachers and teaching assistants in the delivery of services to pupils with Developmental Coordination Difficulties.

What constitutes good partnership working

- A baseline level of knowledge that exists for all health and educational professionals, and information that is understandable and accessible to the parent.
- Early screening by health visitors to highlight developmental delay.
- Regular and reliable contact between parents and professionals.
- Multi-professional/parent observation at assessment to ensure a full picture of the child or adult's difficulties and needs.
- A clear understanding of parental and child/adult expectation so that there is not a delivery mismatch (i.e. what the teacher wants the child to achieve may be very different from what the child wants to achieve).
- Multi-professional/parent discussions about services – with a clear step-wise plan, with appropriate review dates to measure success (this needs to be defined at the outset).
- Mutual acceptance of changes in professional 'power' in varying settings – a sharing rather than protective approach in determining services and support.
- A willingness to review and audit service provision and make appropriate changes.
- Health and education willing to buy from both the top and the bottom.
- Considering the child or adult at the centre of the decision-making process.

Discussion – How can greater collaboration be facilitated between health and educational professionals in meeting the needs of an individual with DCD? What structures are there in place to involve the parents and are they really utilised?

References

Bouffard, M. and Wall, A.E. (1990) 'A problem solving approach to movement skill acquisition: implications for special needs populations', in Reid, G. (ed) *Problems in Movement Control*, North Holland: Elsevier Science.

Gentile, A.M. (1992) 'The nature of skill acquisition: therapeutic implications for children with movement disorders', *Medical Sports Science*, **36**, 31–40.

Hanko, H. (1990) *Special Needs in Ordinary Classrooms: Supporting Teachers*, 2nd edn. Oxford: Blackwell.

Henderson, S.E. and Sugden, D.A. (1992) *Movement Assessment Battery for Children*. The Psychological Corporation.

Keogh, J.F., Sugden, D.A., Reynard, C.L. and Calkins, J.A. (1979) 'Identification of clumsy children: comparisons and comments', *Journal of Human Movement Studies*, **5**, 32–41.

Mandich, A.D., Polatajko, H.J., Macnab, J.J. and Miller, L.T. (2001) 'Treatment of children with Developmental Coordination Disorders. What is the evidence', *Physical and Occupational Therapy in Pediatrics*, **20** (2/3), 51–68.

Orelore, F. and Sobsey, D. (1991) *Educating Children with Multiple Disabilities. A Transdisciplinary Approach*. Baltimore: Paul Brookes.

Polatajko, H.J., Macnab, J.J., Anstett, B., Malloy-Miller, T., Murphy, K. and Noh, S. (1995) 'A clinical trial of the process-oriented treatment approach for children with Developmental Coordination Disorder', *Developmental Medicine and Child Neurology*, **37**, 310–19.

Polatajko, H.J., Mandich, A.D., Miller, L.T. and Macnab, J.J. (2001) 'Cognitive orientation to daily occupational performance (CO-OP): Part II – the evidence', *Physical and Occupational Therapy in Pediatrics*, **20** (2/3), 83–106.

Stephenson, E., McKay, C. and Chesson, R. (1991) 'The identification and treatment of motor/learning difficulties: parents' perceptions and the role of the therapist', *Child: Care, Health and Development*, **17**, 91–113.

Sugden, D.A. and Chambers, M.E. (1998) 'Intervention approaches and children with developmental coordination disorder', *Pediatric Rehabilitation*, **2**, 139–47.

Williams, J. and Unwin, J. (1997) 'Physiotherapy management of minimal cerebral dysfunction in Australia: current practice and future challenges', *Australian Journal of Physiotherapy*, **43**, 135–43.

Glossary of terms

Age Equivalent Score	Refers to the average age at which children receive a given score in the context of standardised tests.
Apraxia	The lack of praxis or motor planning. Interference with planning and executing an unfamiliar task.
Articulation	The production of vowels and consonants by the active and passive articulators in the mouth. The active articulators are the moving parts of the mouth (lips/tongue/soft palate) which can produce sounds while the passive articulators are the non-moving parts of the mouth (hard palate/teeth) against which, in the production of many sounds, the active articulators come into contact.
Asymmetry	One side of the body is different from the other, i.e. one side shorter or more flexed than the other.
ATNR	Asymmetrical Tonic Neck Reflex. A posture adopted with the head and arms in response to stretch applied to the neck muscles, e.g. when the head is turned to the left, the arm and leg on that side extend, while the limbs on the opposite side flex. It should be integrated into the movement system by four months of age.
Auditory	Pertaining to the hearing.
Auditory Discrimination	Difficulties in hearing the differences between words/sounds (e.g. 'f' versus 'v' – 'pat' versus 'bat').
Auditory Memory	The ability to retain and recall verbal information.
Auditory Perceptual Problems	Trouble taking information through the sense of hearing and/or processing that information. The child may hear inaccurately.
Auditory Sequential Memory	The ability to hear a sequence of sounds or words or sentences and be able to hold them in the memory for sufficient time so as to be able to gain information from them, process that information and respond to it.

Augmentative and Alternative Communication Communication systems that may be used as an alternative to speech, or in addition to speech, where their role is to facilitate (or augment) more effective communication. Augmentative and alternative communication systems may be *aided*, where objects, pictures, symbols or writing are used in the form of a chart, book or spoken output device, or *unaided*, where communication is achieved through the use of gesture, mime or signing systems.

Babble A stage in normal spoken language acquisition (from about six months) when the child produces sequences of speech sounds in vocal play, with a shift to more labial and alveolar consonants.

Balance Ability to stay in and regain a position such as standing and sitting.

Bi-lateral The ability to coordinate both sides of the body.

Bi-lateral Integration The ability to move both sides of the body in opposing patterns of movement such as jumping sideways.

Body Percept A person's perception of his or her own body; it consists of sensory pictures or 'maps' of the body stored in the brain. It may also be called the body scheme or body image.

Central Programming Neural functions that are innate within the central nervous system; they do not have to be learned; crawling on hands and knees and walking are good examples of centrally programmed actions.

Cerebral Palsy Permanent, but not unchanging, disorder of posture and movement resulting from brain damage.

Clinical Observations Some testing is done using observation over a period of time rather than formal, timed testing. This does mean there may be inter-observer variation.

Cluttering Rapid and muddled speech.

Co-contraction The simultaneous contraction of all the muscles around a joint to stabilise it.

Communication The act of conveying one's meaning to others. Communication occurs when one person's behaviour is interpreted or inferred as meaningful and understood by their partner in the interaction. Communication may be intentional or unintentional. All communication normally involves the interaction of both verbal and non-verbal components.

Content of Language	Refers to the child's intended meaning.
Cooing	Sounds produced by a baby in the first four months which are largely vocalic (vowels) with an increasing number of velar or 'back' consonantal sounds.
Coordination	Muscles working together to achieve smooth, efficient movements.
Development	Process of growth of all body parts and functions, physical, emotional and intellectual.
Directional awareness	The ability to move in different directions such as forwards, backwards and sideways.
Distractible	Not able to concentrate.
Double blind	The person carrying out the testing and the person being tested are not aware of which type of test is being used – the trial one or the 'inactive' one.
Dysarthria (anarthria)	Difficulty in the articulation of speech sounds, attributable to muscular or neuromuscular defects. Dysarthria comprises a group of speech disorders resulting from disturbances in muscular control. Because there has been damage to the central or peripheral nervous system, some degree of weakness, slowness, uncoordination, or altered muscle tone characterises the activity of the speech mechanism. The term anarthria designates speechlessness due to severe loss of motor function of speech musculature. It is probably the most common symptom of speech disorder in cerebral palsy.
Dyscalculia	A problem with mathematical concepts.
Dyslexia	Difficulty in reading or learning to read.
Dysphagia	Swallowing disorders characterised by difficulty in oral preparation for the swallow or in moving a bolus from the mouth to the stomach. Subsumed in this definition are problems in positioning food in the mouth, including suckling, sucking and mastication.
Dysphasia (Aphasia)	A disturbance of language that can affect both receptive and expressive skills, sometimes one more than the other. It can affect spoken/written or gestured language. Acquired aphasia is a language disorder resulting from localised neurological damage. It may present the individual with difficulties in the perception, recognition, comprehension and expression of language through both the verbal and/or written

	modalities. Also used to refer to developmental language disorder where skills are not being acquired in accordance with the known developmental sequence.
Dyspraxia	Poor praxis or motor planning, a less severe but more common dysfunction than apraxia.
Equilibrium	Refers to body movements or shift in weight in order to regain/maintain balance.
Expressive Language	Communication by means of the spoken word. The ability to produce spoken language that is grammatically/syntactically sound and coherent in both content and sequence.
Extension	The action of straightening, e.g. back, neck, arms or legs.
Eye/Hand Coordination	This is the ability of the eyes and hands to work together, e.g. it is needed for writing.
Finger Agnosia	The ability to recognise which finger is being touched when vision is excluded.
Flexion	The act of bending or pulling in a part of the body.
Floppy	Parts (or all) of the body that feel very loose, and can be moved in a greater range than would be expected.
Form of Language	Refers to the outward aspects of language – the sounds, the syntax and the way in which words are modified to change meaning, e.g. plural or verbalising.
Foundation skills	Skills required for general development, i.e. vision, balance, bi-lateral integration, coordination and motor planning. These skills are necessary at an automatic level in order to learn more complex skills.
Grammar	Refers to the way in which words are and can be combined to make sentences.
Higher Level Language	The ability to process, integrate, interpret and organise verbal/written language.
Hypernasal	Excessive escape of air through the nose, producing a voice such as that often heard in people with cleft palate.
Hyponasal	Reduced passage of air through the nose producing a voice sounding as if the person is 'blocked up' with a bad cold.
IEP	Individual Education Plan for the child with special educational needs.

Information Carrying Words	Refers to those words that carry key information within an utterance.
Intervention	Where a defined procedure by manipulation of the subject or the subject's environment is carried out and data is collected.
Jargon	Expressive language or sound play with normal sounding intonation appropriate to the mother tongue but which does not make sense. There may be a few meaningful words interspersed with the jargon. Prominent from nine months.
Language	A code system used for conveying messages and sharing information among those who know the code. It may be transmitted by speech, writing or gesture. Use of language depends on a receptive channel (comprehension) and an expressive channel. Language is typically described in terms of: (i) Structure: Grammar (syntax), Morphology (the form of words); (ii) Pronunciation: Phonetics, Phonology (the use of sound contrasts to signal meaning); (iii) Meaning (Semantics): semantic = the relationship between words or sentences and their meanings; Vocabulary (meanings of words), Discourse (language in context; functions of language).
Lateral	The aspect of a limb or body part furthest away from the body's midline.
Laterality	The tendency for certain processes to be handled more efficiently on one side of the brain than on the other. In most people the right hemisphere becomes more efficient in processing spatial and musical patterns, while the left specialises in verbal and logical processes.
Laxity	Lack of ligamentous support at joints allowing a wider than average range of movement.
Lumbar	The natural curve of the lower spine.
Medial	The aspect of a limb or body part closest to the body's midline.
Midline	This develops out of laterality. A child needs to have a well-defined midline in order to develop a sense of space around themselves and to be able to orientate themselves to their surroundings.

Motor Planning	The ability of the brain to conceive, organise and carry out a sequence of unfamiliar actions – also known as praxis.
Non-verbal	Refers to all other ways in which children use the context to understand what someone is saying.
Oral Peripheral Examination	The passive and active oral structures are investigated to ascertain the existence of any abnormality. Their function is then determined to ascertain whether any breakdown in the accuracy/speed/sequencing coordination of movement could be contributing to decreased speech intelligibility and/or exacerbating feeding patterns.
Perception	The meaning the brain gives to sensory input.
Perceptual Constancy	The ability to perceive an object as possessing certain properties such as shape, position and size in spite of the different way it may be presented.
Pes Planovalgus	A correctable foot deformity appearing as a flattening of the arches due to lack of ligamentous support and muscle strength.
Phonation	The production of voice by the vibration of the vocal folds (cords) using exhaled air.
Phoneme	Speech sound.
Phonological awareness	The ability to identify numbers and syllables and repeat multi-syllabic words to detect/generate rhymes, to blend and segment words into their component syllables and sounds. These skills are important prerequisites for developing reading, writing and spelling.
Phonology	Refers to the rules that allow children to perceive and produce the differences between sounds in a highly regular manner. These rules are usually acquired within the first three or four years of age.
Physiotherapy	Management of the movement disorders through physical exercise.
Placebo effect	A substance or treatment with no medicinal properties which causes a patient or an individual to improve because of a belief in its efficacy.
Pragmatics	Refers to the child's ability to use language in context. Children may see things literally, be inflexible in their speech and not understand sarcasm, idiom and metaphor.

Prone	Horizontal body position with the face and stomach downward.
Proprioception	From the Latin word 'one's own'. The sensations from the muscles and joints. Proprioceptive input tells the brain when and how the joints are bending, extending or being pulled or compressed. This information enables the brain to know where each part of the body is and how it is moving.
Protective Extension	The reflex that extends the arms to provide protection when the body is falling.
Qualitative	The characteristics, the discovery of regularities; the comprehension of meaning of text or action, and reflection.
Quantitative	The quantitative approach classically tends to assume a clean and deterministic outlook both in analysis and methodology of research; the focus being on producing a hypothesis, indicating how it will be tested, testing it, and verifying or modifying the hypothesis based on the tests carried out.
Raw Score	A term used when counting the number of correct responses on a standardised test. It is usually contrasted with the standard score.
Receptive Language	The ability to understand language.
Reflexes	Always exactly the same response to a certain stimulus, e.g. turning the head to the left causes extension of the limbs on that side, and flexion of limbs on the other side.
Refractive error	The lens power required producing a perfectly focused image on the retina.
Semantics	Refers to meaning conveyed by vocabulary and the grammatical structures that the child uses.
Sensory Input	The stream of electrical impulses flowing from the sense receptors in the body via the spinal cord to the brain.
Sequencing	The ability to master individual steps in an activity and pass from one component part to the next in the correct order.
Skill	The efficiency of carrying out a task.
Spatial Orientation	Knowledge of space and the distance between the self and objects in the environment.

Speech	Spoken language – makes use of phonation and articulation.
Speech and Language Therapy	Management of eating, drinking, speech and language and communication difficulties.
Standard Score	The single most important score derived from a standardised test, this allows us to express the child's performance in terms of where it comes relative to a group of children on whom the test was originally developed.
Stereognosis	The ability to perceive and understand the shape, size and texture of objects by the sense of touch alone.
STNR	Symmetrical Tonic Neck Reflex. Postures adopted by the arms and legs in response to stretch applied to the neck muscles, e.g. when the neck is extended the arms extend while the legs flex. When the head is flexed, the arms collapse into flexion and the legs extend. It should be integrated into movement by four months of age.
Supine	Horizontal body position with face and stomach upward.
Symmetrical Integration	The ability to move both sides of the body simultaneously in identical patterns of movement.
Tactile Defensiveness	A sensory integrative dysfunction in which tactile sensations cause excessive emotional reactions, hyperactivity or other behavioural problems.
Tone	The normal state of readiness of healthy muscle fibres at rest.
Use of Language	Comparable to the term pragmatics and refers to the child's ability to use language in context.
Vestibular System	The sensory input that responds to the position of the head in relation to gravity and decelerated or accelerated movement.
Visual	Pertaining to sight.
Visual Closure	The ability to recognise an object when presented as an incomplete form.
Visual Discrimination	The ability to discriminate similarities and differences in characteristics, arrangements, sequences and organisation of visual stimuli.
Visual Figure Ground	The ability to differentiate a stimulus from its background or the ability to attend to one stimulus without being distracted by irrelevant visual stimuli.

Visual Memory	The ability to recall characteristics of stimuli through vision only.
Visual Motor Integration	The integration of visual motor information which enables eye–hand coordination that is required to carry out activities.
Visual Perception	Judging depth, visual closure, visual discrimination and visual figure ground. Difficulty with visual perception leads to difficulty processing information, seeing the difference between two objects, seeing how far away and how near objects might be.
Visual-Spatial Relationships	The ability to sense the relationship of objects both from each other and from the individual. Depth, length, position, direction and movement are all aspects of this sense.
Winging	Where the shoulder blades stand proud of the chest wall through lack of muscular support.

Recommended reading

Asperger Syndrome Employment Workbook, R. N. Meyer, ISBN 1-85302-796-0.

Asperger Syndrome in the Family, L. Holliday Willey, Jessica Kingsley, ISBN 1-85302-873-8.

Autistic Spectrum Disorders, R. Jordan, David Fulton Publishers, ISBN 1-85346-666-2.

Children with Developmental Co-ordination Disorder – Strategies for Success, C. Missiuna (2001), Haworth Press, ISBN 0-7890-1358-4.

'Clumsy children: a primer on developmental coordination disorder', A.M. Fox and B. Lent (1996), *Canadian Family Physician*, **42**.

Developmental Coordination Disorder, D. Larkin and S.A. Cermak (2002), Albany, New York: Delmar.

Developmental Dyspraxia – Identification and Intervention, 2nd edn, M. Portwood (1999), David Fulton Publishers, ISBN 1-85346-573-9.

Dyslexia and the Workplace, D. Bartlett and S. Moody, ISBN 1-86156-172-5.

Dyslexia in Adults – Education and Employment, G. Reid and J. Kirk, ISBN 0-471-85205-8.

Dyspraxia – A Guide for Teachers and Parents, K. Ripley, B. Daines and J. Barrett (2000), David Fulton Publishers, ISBN1-85346-444-9.

Dyspraxia 5–11 A Practical Guide, C. Macintyre (2001), David Fulton Publishers, ISBN 1-85346-784-7.

Dyspraxia in the Early Years, C. Macintyre (2000), David Fulton Publishers, ISBN 1-85346-677-8.

Dyspraxia, the Hidden Handicap, A. Kirby (1999), Souvenir Press, ISBN 0-285-63512-3.

Helping Children to Build Self-Esteem, D. Plummer, ISBN 1-85302-927-0.

Helping Clumsy Children, N. Gordon and I. McKinlay (1980), New York: Churchill Livingstone.

Improving Behaviour and Raising Self-Esteem in the Classroom – A Practical Guide to Using Transactional Analysis, G. Barrow, E. Bradshaw and T. Newton (2001), David Fulton Publishers, 1-85436-775-8.

Inclusion for Children with Dyspraxia/DCD, K. Ripley (2001), David Fulton Publishers, ISBN 1-85346-762-6.

Incorporating Social Goals in the Classroom, R.A. Moyes, ISBN 1-85302-967-X.

Learning a Living, D.S. Brown, ISBN 0-933149-87-5.

Motor Learning Concepts and Application, 6th edn, R.A. Magill (2001), McGraw-Hill International Editions, ISBN 0-07-118172-5.

Problems in Movement Skill Development, D.A. Sugden and J.F. Keogh (1990), Columbia: University of South Carolina Press.

Scattered Minds: A New Look at the Origins and Healing of Attention Deficit Disorder, G. Mate (1999), Toronto: Knopt, ISBN 0-676-97259-4.

Semantic-Pragmatic Language Disorder, C. Firth and K. Venkatesh, ISBN 0-86388-329-X.

Sensory Integration and the Child, A.J. Ayres (1987), WPS, ISBN 0-87424-158-8.

Sensory Motor Handbook – A Guide for Implementing and Modifying Activities in the Classroom, 2nd edn, J. Bissell, J. Fisher, C. Owens and P. Polcyn (1998), Therapy Skill Builders, ISBN 076-1643-86-9.

Skills Training for Children with Behaviour Disorders: A Parent and Therapist Guidebook, M.L. Bloomquist, Checkmate Plus Books.

Special Educational Needs in the Early Years, R.A. Wilson (1999), Routledge, ISBN 0-41516383-8.

Styles and Learning Strategies – Understanding Style Differences in Learning and Behaviour, R. Riding and S. Rayner (1998), David Fulton Publishers, ISBN 1-85346-480-5.

Survival Strategies for Parenting Children with Bipolar Disorder, G.T. Lynn (2000), Jessica Kingsley.

Talkabout, A. Kelly, ISBN 0-86388-323-0.

Taming the Recess Jungle, C. Gray, ISBN 188547721X.

Teaching Children with Pragmatic Difficulties of Communication, G. Mackay and C. Anderson, David Fulton Publishers, ISBN 1-85346-650-6.

The Explosive Child: A New Approach for Understanding and Parenting Easily Frustrated, 'Chronically Inflexible' Children, R.W. Greene (1998), New York: HarperCollins, ISBN 0060175346.

Treating the Disruptive Adolescent, E.M. Bustamente, ISBN 0-7657-0235-5.

Understanding Developmental Dyspraxia – A Textbook for Students and Professionals, M. Portwood (2000), David Fulton Publishers, ISBN1-85346-574-7.

Understanding Motor Development, 4th edn, D.L. Gallahue and J.C. Ozmun (1998), McGraw-Hill International Editions, ISBN 0-07-115992-4.

Index

Printed in the United Kingdom
by Lightning Source UK Ltd.
124581UK00001B/33-34/A

9 781853 469138